To Cal –

May God bless you.

Mark

Jeremiah 17: 7-8

"When an unexpected tragedy strikes, raw questions always stalk the victims: 'How do I process this, make sense of it, and hardest of all, work my way through this darkness?' The best answer is, not without help. And help is what my friend Mark Saviers so insightfully offers in *Flipped*. Please know there are no pat answers here. This is a riveting story of honest struggle for real answers in the midst of heartache and pain. The good news is Mark delivers real answers. Real answers that will encourage anyone who has either suffered a tragedy personally or been tied tight to one as a family member or friend. I highly recommend it!"

Dr. Robert Lewis
Author, Pastor, Founder-Men's Fraternity

"As a medical oncologist, I have seen lives flipped on a daily basis for 30 years. Whether suddenly getting a cancer diagnosis or falling from a ladder with resulting quadriplegia, life is immediately redefined. What Tommy and company show us through his powerful and compelling story, becomes the best practical manual I've ever seen for what to do when tragedy strikes. The personal courage that comes only from the confident knowledge that God's love is magnified by difficult circumstances, is personified through Tommy as he becomes a beacon of light to all who come in to contact with him. The joyful sacrifice of his wife, Robyn, family and friends, in whom God's love and purpose overwhelm anger and resentment each day, show us exactly what Christ had in mind for being his heart on this earth. Anyone thrown into flipped in their own life will find reading this book is an incredible guide to glorifying God, understanding His love in tragedy and demonstrating the very nature of victory through faith, hope, and love."

Dr. Lawrence Mendelsohn, Medical Oncologist
Founding Medical Director of The CARTI Regional Cancer Center, Little Rock, AR

"*Flipped* is a firsthand account of the far-reaching effects of a catastrophic injury to the entire family. It is a story of perseverance and courage. It is a journey of faith and trusting that God is present during the most chaotic of times. While this offering centers around Tommy, it also details how roles in the family change in order to survive the challenges of a spinal cord injury. It is a reminder that we are to live out Jesus' calling of loving our neighbor even when it disrupts our daily lives."

Candi Boyd, MDiv.
Chaplain, Craig Hospital

"I have been privileged to know Tommy for forty years. I have never seen a more heroic, loving person, who genuinely cares more about everyone else than he does himself. God has given him peace. And God has given him purpose. If you need hope, read *Flipped*. If you need inspiration, read *Flipped*. If you want to see a wife, sons, family and friends trust God through indescribable adversity, read *Flipped*. Most of all, if you want to truly see God at work, read *Flipped*!"

David Roth
President and CEO, Workmatters

"Tommy Van Zandt's accident could have broken his family into pieces. Instead, it pulled them together. This book provides a unique and raw perspective on how God can turn tragedies into triumph."

Stephen R. Graves
Author and Founder of Coaching By Cornerstone

"Tommy and Robyn Van Zandt are bright lights shining in a world that needs much more illumination about things that really matter. In business and community life, their passion for excellence and love for others truly sets them apart and inspires the rest of us to live and lead as they do. When I am in need of perspective and wisdom, I often find myself calling upon Tommy and Robyn. Now their invaluable teachings are available through this book and will provide a roadmap for many others to follow."

Elise Mitchell, Chairman, Mitchell Communications Group
CEO, Dentsu Aegis Public Relations Network

"Thank you for asking me to read this powerful and moving account of God working in and through tragedy. Dietrich Bonhoeffer, if I recall correctly, said, 'Christ never calls a person but what he calls them to come and die.' This is a phenomenal story of selfless love and devotion by an entire family in Christ. It is a powerful, moving, and real-life testimony to God's mysterious ways of loving us and guiding us to love and stand alongside one another. This book will be helpful to anyone, including the soldiers returning with the wounds of war."

Jim Daniel
Brigadier General (Retired) USA, Chairman, Darby's Warrior Support

"I could not put this book down. From the first word to the last I found the book to be gripping, authentic, and honest with stories shared from the heart about dealing with a spinal cord injury. *Flipped* will help families navigate those first few days while in shock as well as the long-term plans that will need to be addressed. Most of all this book shares hope reminding us that miracles from God to happen—the true miracle is the Spirit and Strength God gives us all to face each day. God's steadfast love endures forever."

Cindy Burns, M. Ed.
Counselor, Shepherd Spinal Center, 1982-85

"I marvel at *Flipped* for its inspiration, humor and courage, as well as the riveting stories of life's vicissitudes in the face of tragedy. The utter dependence on God's grace shines brightly from these pages. I read it through the lens of a father who has experienced the ravages of the opioid epidemic, which recently claimed the life of our precious youngest son and has wreaked havoc on another. This account of how Jesus, family, and community guide us through unspeakable hardship will be a profound blessing to many, as it was for me."

Rainer Twiford
Founder and President, Brookline Investments

FLIPPED

How one man's
tragic fall became a story of
surrender, **faith**, and **hope**.

Mark Saviers

With reflections by Robyn and Tommy Van Zandt

Without Vicki, my wife, best friend, and soul mate, this story could not be the same and my life would not be the same. Vicki has enriched every part of my being for forty-three years—and counting. And to all of the many wonderful people who have offered prayers, time, and talents to lift up and sustain the Van Zandt family—we will never forget what you have done. We are eternally grateful. We prayed for miracles, and one of them was you.

Table of Contents

Foreword

Paralyzed by ... Life
By Tommy and Robyn Van Zandt

Before you dive into this book, take a few seconds and do a short mental exercise.

There's a word you need to keep in mind as you read this story, a word that's central to the theme in ways that are obvious but also in ways you probably won't expect. So before you begin, do us (and yourself) a favor and say this one word out loud: *Paralysis.*

Think about it. Let it soak in to your mind and your soul. Say it out loud again. Reflect on what it means to you and why.

Paralysis.

It's a scary word, isn't it?

Here's the way it's described by *Merriam-Webster:* "complete or partial loss of function especially when involving the motion or sensation in a part of the body ... loss of the ability to move ... a state of powerlessness or incapacity to act."[1]

Scary, indeed.

But here's the thing: The body isn't the only thing that suffers from paralysis. There's also emotional paralysis and, worst of all, spiritual paralysis.

We live every day with the reality of physical paralysis— one of us (Tommy) is a quadriplegic and the other (Robyn) is his spouse and primary caregiver. It's not the life we chose,

---

1. *Merriam-Webster.com Dictionary,* s.v. "paralysis," accessed August 21, 2017, https://www.merriam-webster.com/dictionary/paralysis.

but it's the life we've been given. And it's the life you'll read about in this book.

We can tell you, because we've seen it and lived it, that there are far worse things than physical paralysis. Emotional paralysis will cripple your relationships. And we can't imagine anything much worse than spiritual paralysis —it will torture your soul.

So we hope you will find in these pages a message for transcending paralysis, no matter what form it might take.

We all get stuck in life from time to time, and some of those times can last pretty long. Something bad happens—something we do or something happens that's beyond our control—and we get knocked for a loop.

Our life gets flipped.

We get frustrated and angry—at ourselves, at the people we love the most, at God. We get drawn into that dark place where moving forward, just taking one step, seems like the most impossible thing on earth.

We become paralyzed by our pride or our fears. Unable to function effectively. Unable to move in a positive direction. Powerless to act for the good of ourselves or others.

Scary becomes our constant reality.

Thankfully, here's the greater reality: There is always a way forward. There is life and hope in the midst of tragedy. No matter how your life has been flipped, you can get up, you can move on, and, most of all, you can experience the joy and peace that God provides.

This book tells our family's story, and, yes, it's a story of tragedy and paralysis. But most of all, we believe it's a story of surrender, faith, and hope—gifts from God that have sustained us and continually shine through the darkness in the lives of our friends, family, and community.

As you'll see in the pages that follow, we often didn't handle our tragedy well. We still don't always handle it very well. On our own, we never will. With God, however, all things are possible. He didn't create us to leave us alone in our tragedies; He helps us and heals us in the midst of them.

We are driven by the belief that everyone's life matters. Our lives matter. Your life matters. As humans, we are all created by and for God. We are not an accident, not one of us. Our lives are to be valued, to be respected, to be acknowledged. Who we are and how we were created—that's enough.

This realization is both incredibly affirming and humbling.

Spending time trying to prove we are better than others, deserve more, or are somehow more special than others never works. In fact, it ultimately makes us feel less worthy, less special. It keeps us from the meaningful connections that help us become our best selves. It leads to paralysis in our hearts.

Life on this earth is not meant to be easy, but it is meant to bring joy. We are meant to grow, learn, deeply appreciate, and love other humans and what creation has to offer—when life is smooth, and especially when life is challenging.

Tragedy is not a journey we should ever take alone. When we take it with loved ones and friends and, most of all, with God, then courage is always within our reach and giving up is never an option. The tragedy is no less real, no less painful, but the tragedy never wins.

So, no matter what type of tragedy you face—no matter what form of paralysis is taking a grip on you physically, emotionally, or spiritually—we hope this book will give you the courage, faith, and hope to live in the grace and joy of God.

Introduction

Flipped in an Instant

We were desperate.

When Tommy Van Zandt fell off a ladder and broke his neck in February 2009, not only did his life change in a split second, so did the lives of everyone in our family.

Tommy is my business partner, lifelong friend, and brother-in-law. At forty-nine, he had a truly wonderful life, complete with a happy marriage and two bright, healthy teenage sons. But in the blink of an eye, an accident left him near death and paralyzed below the neck. Everything he and his family had built suddenly seemed in jeopardy, and the future had never looked more terrifying.

His life had been flipped.

Our lives had been flipped.

Yes, we were desperate, but I knew God would help us. I had no idea how or when, but I knew He would sustain us in His own way and in His own time.

I began recording this story immediately after learning of Tommy's accident, writing it by hand in a journal every two or three days for a year, because I knew God would take action. The initial idea was simply to capture all the details of our journey and how God would work in our lives. I wrote it so our family would never forget all of the miracles I felt certain we would experience.

But as the story unfolded day by day over months, it occurred to me that other people dealing with personal tragedies might benefit from knowing what happened to us. Maybe it will give others hope.

Our family is like many others, just ordinary people

dealing with an unusual tragedy. Sadly, most families have some kind of tragedy. Many have incredibly difficult situations. But we all have one thing in common: A God who loves us and cares deeply about what happens to us. There is always hope.

So time moved on, and six years after Tommy's accident, we edited my notes and added the goal of sharing it with others. I wanted to give God glory for helping us. I wanted to illustrate the power of faithful family and friends coming together during difficult times. And I wanted to communicate the inspiration that Tommy and his wife, Robyn, continue to be to everyone around them. Hopefully this book will help them widen their ministry.

Today, Tommy lives a normal life—but it's his normal, not yours or mine.

He's a quadriplegic. He requires twenty-four-hour care from Robyn and paid caregivers. He can't turn his head to look at you. But stand in front of him, and he will look you squarely in the eyes. He will talk to you and laugh with you. He will make jokes at his own expense and, if he knows you, at yours as well. He works about twenty hours a week. He goes to church. He goes out to dinner. With the help of his caregivers, he sends e-mails and makes phone calls. And he shares the love and joy God has placed in his heart with anyone who will listen.

To some, he looks rather helpless, and it's true there are many things he can't do on his own. But what he does for others is nothing short of amazing. He contributes at work, to his family, to his community, and to others with his insights, his humor, and his attitude.

Robyn remains steadfastly by his side, managing their home and his care. She also remains close to her friends and works parttime coaching others through the trials of life, a topic with which she's intimately familiar.

Together, whether it's mentoring individuals or speaking to groups at events, Tommy and Robyn regularly share an inspiring message about trusting God and persevering through the trials of life.

Their sons, Ross and Jack, are adults now, forging their path in the world. But they are forever connected to the events of 2009, events that shaped their lives and the lives of everyone connected to Tommy.

This book is our family's story, but more than that, it's a God story. It's not just my story. It's not just the Van Zandt's story. It's a whole community's story.

While it's based on one year of my journal, there is a retrospective passage at the end of each chapter from Tommy or Robyn, so they could share their thoughts while looking back to that time. I also include thoughts from a variety of other sources collected during that first year—e-mails, blog entries, and notes from friends, family, and a few people we barely know at all. So, it's also a story about the goodness of people—about a huge community who came together to help a family in need.

To understand this story, however, a little background on our family will be helpful.

My name is Mark Saviers, and I grew up in Fort Smith, Arkansas. Coming from a wholesome family with a large network of friends, Fort Smith was good to me. My father (Pop) is a retired surgeon who is ninety-three. He met my mother when she was a beautiful young nurse working in a hospital in Indianapolis. They settled in Fort Smith to raise three children: my older brother, Jim; my younger sister, Ann; and me.

We lived what now seems like an episode of *Leave It to Beaver*—a simple, hardworking, and loving life. Until my mother got sick with breast cancer at age sixty-four, I had never really experienced hardship. So, for many years, I didn't realize how much I was blessed. I was a living example of being "born on third base and thought I had hit a triple."

When I was in the eighth grade, I became good friends with Vicki Van Zandt, who later became the love of my life. We dated steadily from our senior year in high school through college, and we married between our junior and senior years at the University of Arkansas.

Vicki has one sibling, a younger brother, Tommy. When I started hanging around their house in the eighth grade, Tommy was ten years old and in the fourth grade. He latched onto me because he had no big brother.

I liked him, too. He was hilarious. He had a big, curly head of hair that, at the time, was not "the look" he wanted. So, he ran around his house with a wet head covered by a stocking cap, trying to make his hair lay down straight before he went outside. He followed Vicki and me around, spying on us. His father, Jerry, who would become known as "Big Dad" by his grandkids, didn't fish much, so Tommy tagged along with me. As he got a little older, I taught him to duck hunt, too. Tommy became like my younger brother.

Vicki and Tommy's mother, Annella, picked up the nickname "Mud" from her grandchildren. When her first grandchild was born, she wanted to be called "Mudder," slang for Mother and a nickname used by another grandmother in the family. Over time, her grandkids morphed it into Mud, Mud-Doo, and Muddy. Now she's called Mud by everyone in the family.

She was always very kind to me, even though, as I look back now, I realize I must have driven her crazy hanging around her house so much. She and Jerry were several years younger than my parents. They were full of life, laughter, and fun. I loved their whole family, which is why I spent so much time with them.

Tommy would follow Vicki and me to the University of Arkansas. Naturally, I wanted him to pledge Phi Delta Theta, the fraternity where I had made so many friends, some of whom are mentioned later in this book.

Tommy had visited us at the U of A while he was still in high school, so he knew a lot of Phi Delts, too, and later pledged there. This pleased me, of course, so I gladly bestowed upon him my most treasured piece of Phi Delta Theta memorabilia—my homemade Viking Party hat. It was a Tupperware bowl covered in faux brown fur and sporting the horns of a cow that had been screwed or glued onto it. It was magnificent. You'd have thought I had given Tommy ten bars of gold. Over the next four years, we saw the hat appear in many party pictures—and not just on Tommy.

After graduation, Vicki and I started our careers in Little Rock. She worked for the Pulaski County Election Commission, and I worked at IBM. Soon, IBM transferred us to Fort Smith, where both of our sons were born. Marshall arrived in 1980, and John Mark followed in 1982. They were, and are, our pride and joy.

After five years with IBM, I took a job in Dallas with the Trammell Crow Company, a national commercial real estate development firm. Our sons were two years old and two months old.

We lived in six cities and eight houses or apartments during the first thirteen years we were married. The excitement and challenge of commercial real estate suited my personality, while Vicki was the rock of our family as a superb mother and supportive wife.

After our boys went off to college, Vicki shared her talents with many organizations, including establishing the Public Education Foundation in Little Rock and later serving in a governor-appointed position on the Arkansas State Board of Education. Her passion is working to ensure every child, regardless of race or background or means, has an opportunity for a good education.

While Vicki and I were on our trek around the country, Tommy had graduated from the University of Arkansas with a degree in marketing (just like me). His first job was with Phillips Petroleum, where he learned to sell. He told us funny stories about driving around Oklahoma with his boss, who was nicknamed Porky.

After a few years, Tommy moved to Dallas, where he, too, went into commercial real estate. He started with Bright Real Estate, then moved after a few years to Transwestern Property Company. Transwestern grew rapidly for the next ten years, as did Tommy's career. The friends he made at Transwestern became the nucleus of the people who hosted the first benefit for the Van Zandt family after his accident.

While Tommy was working in Dallas, he was asked to interview an applicant for an administrative position. In walked Robyn Sims, a beautiful young woman who would become his wife. Robyn had grown up in Mississippi and, after graduating from the University of Texas, moved to Dallas to start her career.

A brief courtship led to their wedding in Dallas. It was a fun and happy occasion that featured a big guest list of Robyn's friends and Tommy's Phi Delta Theta brothers, along with numerous Dallas friends. Their sons, Ross and Jack, were born a few years later in Dallas.

Our last move with Trammell Crow Company was to Chicago, where we lived for more than three years. But as our sons were about to enter the third and fifth grades, we moved back to Arkansas. Vicki helped me realize that the boys needed to be in Arkansas, where both of our parents still lived. She felt strongly that it was time to settle down "back home" so our sons could really get to know our extended family.

It made no sense to me to move, because my job was in Chicago. Looking back, I believe God was urging Vicki to bring us home so we could help our family through the difficult times to come. Within two years, my mother contracted breast cancer and Vicki's father (Big Dad) had a major stroke, leaving him paralyzed on his right side. Mom lived nine more years, and Big Dad lived fifteen years after the onset of these illnesses. We wouldn't take anything now for the blessing of having our sons around them during those years and for the opportunity for all of us to help our parents during challenging times.

Since my job with Trammell Crow was still in Chicago, I kept a car parked at O'Hare International Airport and clothes stored at a Marriott Courtyard while I commuted back and forth each week. Business was booming, making it hard to walk away. The routine lasted eighteen months before I resigned and partnered with Jim Irwin to form Irwin & Saviers Company, an Arkansas-based commercial real estate firm.

Naturally, I was greatly excited when Tommy contacted me, expressing a desire to come home to Arkansas to continue his real estate career at our Fayetteville office.

A few years later, in 2006, Irwin & Saviers split into two companies. One was Sage Partners, which Tommy, Brian Shaw, and I founded. Later, our son Marshall joined us, too, after his own successful stint with Transwestern in Dallas and soon became one of our senior partners. We were all home in Arkansas, working together, and it was very gratifying to all of us.

Life wasn't necessarily perfect for our family in 2009, but it was very, very good. So, when Tommy fell off that ladder and broke his neck, you can imagine the devastation we all felt. This book will take you through the very difficult story of Tommy's injury and the impact it had on all of us around him that first year when our lives were drastically "flipped."

The experiences we've gone through as a family because of his injury have impacted just about every area of our lives. Our relationships, our finances, our faith ... they've all been tested, challenged, and stretched. And while we've all stumbled and occasionally fallen, one thing has remained true: God has carried us through. As Tommy put it, "God doesn't cause bad things to happen, but God is there to pick you up when bad things do happen."

Hopefully, this story about an imperfect family's journey will inspire the type of faith and hope God has given us in the face of Tommy's tragic accident. It's the faith and hope the psalmist expressed and the same type of urgent plea that our family and friends prayed in hundreds of forms and styles:

Hear my cry, O God; listen to my prayer. From the ends of the earth I call to you, I call as my heart grows faint; lead me to the rock that is higher than I. For you have been my refuge, a strong tower against the foe. ... Then I will ever sing in praise of your name and fulfill my vows day after day. (Psalm 61:1–3, 8, NIV)

Chapter 1

A Winter Fall

God is our refuge and strength, an ever-present help in trouble.
Therefore we will not fear, though the earth give way and the
mountains fall into the heart of the sea.
PSALM 46:1–2 (NIV)

The accident occurred about 12:30 p.m. on Saturday, February 7, 2009, but we didn't hear about it until later that day when we were sitting down for dinner.

In an age of fast-paced, constant communication, we had picked this week to get about as far away as possible from the hustle and bustle of the regular world. We weren't totally off the grid, but we were on the edge—away on a once-in-a-lifetime family adventure in a remote area about an hour north of Córdoba, Argentina.

Spending time with family has always been important to Vicki and me, so we were thrilled to travel to South America with our sons, Marshall and John Mark; Marshall's wife, Beth; and Melissa Nutt, John Mark's girlfriend at the time. We planned to dove hunt and sightsee and create memories, but we didn't plan on the phone call that rocked our family's world.

Life felt pretty much perfect as we gathered for dinner that night. Then the outfitter came to the table and asked me to call my sister, Ann, as soon as possible. Vicki and I climbed a staircase to the highest point in the hunting camp so we could get a cell phone signal. With each step, I worried that something had happened to my father, then eighty-five. But when I got on the line, Ann told me Tommy had fallen from a ladder while cutting tree limbs around his home in the aftermath of an ice storm in Fayetteville.

The injuries were serious, Ann said, and Tommy's mother wanted us to know about it right away. The details were sketchy. She thought maybe a branch had fallen and hit Tommy in the head, but it appeared the major injury was a broken neck.

My thoughts raced: *How could this happen?* I wondered. *Tommy is in great shape and quite nimble for a guy forty-nine years old. How could he have been flipped to the point that it would break his neck?*

I hung up and hugged Vicki in the darkness, stunned by the news. In that moment, we were unsure if Tommy would live or die, but we knew we had to cut our trip short. Only thirty-two hours into a ten-day trip that we had planned for two years, we asked the outfitter for help evaluating flight options.

The six of us, meanwhile, prayed for Tommy around a campfire. It was hard to compose myself enough to offer the prayer. I had already broken down hard alone and inside the privacy of our room. Pretending to go to the bathroom, I had leaned my head against the wall and pounded the wall with my forearm, groaning out loud.

Everyone wanted to go home. After much debate,

however, the kids listened to our logic that it would be hard enough to find two emergency tickets, much less six. If they needed to come home right behind us, we promised we would get word to them and help book their flights.

The outfitter spent a couple of hours working on our flight, talking first to his home office and then to the airlines, switching between Spanish and English. The next morning Vicki and I left the rest of our family in the camp's parking lot in Argentina, waving goodbye with all of us near tears.

We drove a Jeep to Córdoba, then flew to Buenos Aires, then to Dallas, and finally back to Little Rock. By the time we showered and drove the three hours to Fayetteville, we had been traveling about thirty-six hours straight. All along the way, we prayed and worried about Tommy and his family: Robyn, his wife of twenty-two years; Ross, who was seventeen and a junior in high school; and Jack, who was barely fourteen and in the eighth grade.

We were especially concerned for Tommy and Vicki's mother, Mud. She adores her children and grandchildren, especially Tommy. We had always teased her about how much she compared everything done by any male in our family to him.

And she had already dealt with too much tragedy. She had cared for her husband, Jerry (Big Dad), for about fifteen years after his stroke and resulting paralysis, and Tommy's accident happened barely a year after Jerry's death. Before her husband's illness, Mud had cared for her mother for several years while she was sick and in a nursing home.

She had given the best part of her adult life to caring for her mother and husband, and we had always admired her for it. Nobody deserved to go through suffering like this with her only son, and we knew it would be particularly hard for Mud.

Vicki and I started working the phone while still in Buenos Aires, trying to better understand Tommy's condition to help determine what would be best for his care.

The ambulance had taken him to Washington Regional Medical Center in Fayetteville. Tommy had a variety of injuries, and it was weeks before I even learned about some of them (like his broken arm). That's because the immediate concern was the life-threatening damage to his spine.

The doctors had scheduled an eight-hour surgery for Monday, February 9, to stabilize Tommy's back, clean up his shattered fifth vertebra (C5), and repair his broken C6 vertebra.

This was the only expected major surgery, so naturally we wanted to learn more about Luke Knox, the neurosurgeon. Jim Counce, a friend of the family and a regionally acclaimed cardiovascular surgeon who lives in Fayetteville, had told another family member that Dr. Knox was excellent and that he would trust his own family member with him. That statement carried a lot of weight with us.

As a board member for Arkansas Children's Hospital in Little Rock, I had become friends with Dr. Jon Bates (CEO) and Dr. Richard Jacobs (chairman of the Department of Pediatrics), so we also sought their advice. Dr. Jacobs called his friend Dr. Rick McCarthy, another fine neurosurgeon in Little Rock, to describe the planned procedure and ask about Dr. Knox and Washington Regional. He also provided Dr. McCarthy's cell phone number so we could call him directly.

I knew Dr. McCarthy would have detailed questions

about Tommy's condition that we could not answer, so Robyn gave me the cell number of Dr. Wayne Brooks, a rehab doctor and close family friend who knew all of the details of the injury. Within two hours, Dr. McCarthy had talked to Dr. Brooks and assured us that the surgical procedure was the best course of action and that Dr. Knox was fully competent to perform it.

All of this happened on a Sunday afternoon while we waited for our flight at the Buenos Aires airport. The Lord was already using many people to help us make the proper decisions. And He would continue to help, one decision and one step at a time.

By the time we landed in Little Rock on Monday, February 9 (my birthday), we knew the surgery had been delayed. For some reason, Tommy's blood was thin, creating a significant risk for such a long surgery.

At first, the doctors delayed the procedure for a few hours. Then to the next day. Then another day. Each day we hoped and prayed for Tommy to begin healing, even while he (and we) waited. Our hearts were filled with hope, but that didn't erase the uncertainty. This husband, father, brother, son, and friend, who had always been such a picture of humor and strength, now lay immobilized—first in a halo device, then in a neck brace—with a feeding and ventilator tube taped into his closed mouth.

And so we waited and prayed.

REFLECTIONS: SEVEN YEARS LATER

By Tommy Van Zandt

It had been about ten days since the big ice storm, and the temperatures had warmed back up. Everyone in town had a lot of trees and tree limbs down, so we were taking advantage of the nice weather on a Saturday and working to clean up the mess Mother Nature had created.

I was on a ten-foot ladder, and I was standing one rung down from the top. I was reaching up high, so my head was maybe fifteen feet in the air when I lost my balance. They think I fell straight back and landed on the back of my head and base of my skull. I fell on the soft ground, but I hit in that perfect spot, and I actually heard my bone break.

At that moment, I felt God's hand on me. Obviously, I was in no pain because of the shock. But I felt God's presence with me. I can tell you that His hand was on my shoulder from the very beginning. It was OK.

I was conscious throughout all of this and fully coherent. When I hit the ground, I knew my neck was broken. But I didn't panic. I was calm, and it was almost funny. In fact, my initial thought was, *Well, your neck is broken. What now, big boy?*

It seemed like a long time, but it was just a matter

of seconds. I felt almost like a soft slow breeze that went over my body bringing paralysis. It was probably the shock. As soon as my neck broke, I'm sure I was paralyzed. But in my mind, it felt as though this breeze went over my body in a *swoosh* and I was paralyzed. So, with that same smart-aleck sense of humor, I said, "Well, you're paralyzed."

I was probably seventy-five yards from our house. Robyn and the boys had come out and helped me cut limbs, but they had gone inside because we had talked about going to eat lunch. I stayed behind. I had to get this one last limb.

I knew I wasn't able to run up and grab anybody, so I started praying very hard that they would come find me. As I was praying, my diaphragm started to paralyze. My breaths became shorter and shorter, so my praying became much more focused.

"God, I am fine going now," I said. "If this is my time, I'm fine with it, but I want to see Robyn and the boys one more time. Please let me see Robyn and the boys one more time."

Just then, Robyn and Jack, our youngest son, came running down the hill.

"Call 911," I said. "My neck is broken."

Robyn ran to make the call, and Jack stayed with me. I was in a fetal position on the ground, and I felt if Jack could get me upright somehow, it would take some pressure off my lungs. He got me up a little on my knees. I was still in a fetal position, but that helped me get a breath or two. It seemed like two seconds later, the EMS truck was in the backyard.

I was in some form of shock and not 100 percent coherent after that. I remember being in the EMS truck with my boys. I was joking and laughing with them and telling them, "Guys, the main thing I want you to do in your lives is laugh and be happy." And I was smiling.

Robyn tells me none of that actually happened. The boys went to the hospital with a family friend, and Robyn rode in the front seat of the ambulance. Nobody was in the truck with me except the medical people. It was something I made up in my mind or something I told them that later got mixed up in my memory.

When I got to the hospital, they put me under and I don't remember any of it. Well, I remember two things, and I don't know which happened first. I remember Mark meeting with me about all the issues of my health, but I was in and out of it. And I remember Robyn walking into the hospital room. They had me in a halo, where they put the thing around your skull to hold your head in place. I remember her coming into the room with a big smile and saying this is all going to be all right. She was smiling, and that gave me the biggest sense of relief and hope.

Chapter 2

The Waiting Game

Be strong and courageous. Do not be afraid;
do not be discouraged, for the LORD your God will be
with you wherever you go.
JOSHUA 1:9 (NIV)

From the moment word began to spread about Tommy's injury, the support of friends, family, and community was overwhelming.

People from Arkansas are family- and relationship-oriented, unusually so, based on our experiences in other places. The waiting room at Washington Regional's ICU was crammed from early morning until late in the evening that first week. It was like a daily sixteen-hour cocktail party, but without the cocktails. Food and soft drinks were everywhere, there was a sign-in book, and people met each other or renewed friendships while waiting together.

Deborah Broyles, one of Tommy and Robyn's close friends, coordinated a schedule for the meals that were awaiting us as we arrived home exhausted each night for the next few weeks. Friends Jill and Trey Hollis created a blog and updated it daily with fresh news and encouraging Scriptures. It became a lifesaver in disseminating information and receiving messages from family and friends all over the country.

The blog served its purpose: "To keep friends of Tommy current on his road to recovery." The verse in the header of the blog provided a much-needed daily reminder of the approach God wants us to take in life: "Be strong and courageous. Do not be afraid; do not be discouraged, for the LORD your God will be with you wherever you go" (Joshua 1:9, NIV). It was especially relevant as we endured a weeks-long waiting game that kept Tommy at Washington Regional far longer than anyone expected.

The first post on the blog was Sunday, February 8, 2009, the day after the accident:

From friendsoftommyv.blogspot.com
As most of you know, on Saturday Feb. 7th, Tommy Van Zandt fell from a ladder while trimming trees in their backyard. Tommy sustained considerable damage to his neck and spinal cord. Tommy never lost consciousness and his breathing has been stable, which is a great blessing. Praise God there was no damage to Tommy's brain! Yesterday, the doctors stabilized his neck and back with halo traction equipment. This morning an MRI confirmed severe bruising to the spinal cord. The result of this damage at the current time is paralysis below the shoulders.

Your overwhelming prayers are sustaining his family and friends. Your prayers are increasing the hope of recovery.

Tomorrow morning, Tommy will go in for surgery at 7:30 a.m. to permanently stabilize his neck. This will be a 6- to 7-hour surgery.

Following this current treatment, Tommy will most likely be taken to Baylor Medical Center in Dallas for rehabilitation.

Above all, please pray for:

(1) Blood flow to return to the spinal cord and spinal cord healing

(2) No complications during and after surgery

(3) Wisdom for Dr. Knox (his surgeon)

(4) Peace and comfort for the family

(5) God's miraculous hand to be at work

For the next two weeks, meals are being provided by the Van Zandts' supper club. As we near the end of this two-week period, we will reanalyze the need for meals and let those who would like to help know what is needed. (e-mail Debra Broyles if you are interested in preparing meals ...)

Posted by Jill and Trey at 4:31 PM

Most of the posts over the next few weeks were informational updates. With each decision to postpone the surgery, a post went up. When Jill and Trey learned something, like how people could e-mail Tommy and Robyn at the hospital, they wrote a post.

On Monday, February 9, the day the surgery originally was scheduled, Jill and Trey posted four or five updates, one of which really captured Tommy's spirit and fight. At the time, Tommy was mostly limited to blinking to communicate since the breathing tube kept him from speaking.

Here's what the post said:

Tommy continues to communicate his desire for everyone to smile. Knowing Tommy, this will not surprise you!

One of Tommy's doctors requested high-top tennis shoes for Tommy to wear in order to keep his feet in good position. In an attempt to return the joy Tommy is so readily giving out, the Shermans went out and bought bright red Converse high tops, which friends then signed with Scripture and love notes. We feel sure this will bring a smile to his face and heart! Prayer: (1) Praise God for Tommy's incredible attitude and strength (2) Praise God for the friends that are bringing joy and comfort (3) Praise God for His trustworthiness and goodness (4) Praise God for His hand at work in taking care of every detail on Tommy's road to healing.

"For I know the plans I have for you," declares the LORD, "plans to prosper you and not to harm you, plans to give you hope and a future." (Jeremiah 29:11)

Posted by Jill and Trey at 8:37 PM

Jill and Trey almost always included some piece of Scripture to offer hope and encouragement. And many people used the blog site to send Scriptures along with personal messages, and even some jokes, all of which were welcomed and were encouraging. It was very hard to return all of the calls and e-mails (and impossible for Robyn), but we certainly appreciated the love we felt.

THE SURGERY

By the end of the first week, the adrenaline that had sustained us was wearing off, and frustration had set in. Tommy had a low-grade fever that added another reason to delay his surgery. Dr. Knox had said he would not operate if Tommy's fever was 101 or above. And when I left the hospital on Sunday night, eight days after the accident, Tommy's fever was still 100.1 and climbing.

I prayed hard on the way home that God would allow this surgery to happen the next day. I told Him we were losing energy and that I was afraid Tommy was slipping away in all of the complications he was experiencing.

God helped us. Tommy's fever remained below the neurosurgeon's threshold, and the surgery was performed February 16. Friends and family crowded the ICU waiting room over the six or so hours of the operation. A grandfatherly chaplain came out of the operating room periodically to tell us all was going well, which we greatly appreciated.

We were all excited to finally get on with it, so there was an anticipation and excitement in the air. Marshall and his wife, Beth, walked in from the long overnight flight back from Argentina just as the news came from the operating room that the surgery had been successfully completed. Everyone did high fives at the news.

During the surgery, Dr. Knox inserted a titanium rod to support Tommy's back and "cleaned up" the vertebrae damage. We later heard that Dr. Knox had said he was "proud of himself" that the spine was now straight. I felt like it was a very good sign for a surgeon of Dr. Knox's caliber and experience to make this statement. We also were delighted to hear his report that the dura mater, a thick protective membrane around the spine, was intact. This could bode well to facilitate healing and to avoid infection.

Tommy recovered well from this major operation, and within a few days we were all ready to move toward breathing exercises to try to get him off the ventilator.

Betty Adkins, a kind but precocious nurse, was his respiratory therapist at Washington Regional. She pushed him to try to "click" his respirator from his own breathing initiative. The first morning she coaxed him, he did three clicks. I told him that was good, but I expected five in the afternoon. He looked at me with a "that's easy for *you* to say" look in his eyes. He did eight clicks in the afternoon to prove he could. The next morning, he did ten, and then he did eighteen in the afternoon. His determination was impressive, and we were all encouraged.

Over the next several days, however, it became clear that although Tommy was trying hard, he was not close to being able to get off the ventilator. The feeding and breathing tube taped into his mouth was very uncomfortable for him. Since he needed to stay on the ventilator for at least a while, a tracheotomy or "trachea" would be necessary soon. This surgical opening in his windpipe would provide direct access for a breathing tube, offer him comfort, and help avoid potential complications by allowing the removal of the feeding tube from his mouth. It would also accelerate the opportunity to move him to a specialty hospital for his rehab.

Time was wearing on. It had been more than two weeks since the accident, but Dr. Knox wanted to make sure the trachea did not cause complications with a wound on Tommy's upper chest that was still healing from the initial surgery.

Again, we had to wait.

TURNING ON A SWITCH

We talked a lot during this time of waiting about how the Israelites waited on God's direction as Moses led them in the desert. God provided a cloud by day or a fire by night when it was time to move. Otherwise, they waited. So we were to wait. And we continually prayed that God would begin Tommy's healing process, believing that He was not dependent on the next medical steps.

During this period, an interesting person named Katinka came to help Tommy. She was very kind and practiced a kind of "alternative medicine." Her technique was an unusual blend of adjusting Tommy's feet, saying key words for him to think about, lightly massaging his skin on his arms or feet, and playing music. The idea is that the body has mysterious healing powers not detected by traditional medicine.

Katinka's father, who moved her and her family from South Africa to Northwest Arkansas, had taught her this technique. It had worked on a former patient of Dr. Knox's who had a head injury, so he did not object. As the son of a surgeon, I must admit to being skeptical. But Katinka told us Tommy's body was telling her that it would heal, and this was an encouraging message. She never charged us, and her presence seemed to make both Robyn and Tommy feel better.

God always seemed to provide that type of encouragement when we were frustrated and really needed it.

On Saturday night, February 21, Tommy and Robyn's spirits were low. The slow progress was wearing on everyone, and it was natural for doubts about Tommy's healing to creep in and to discourage.

On this night, a couple walked into the ICU unannounced and introduced themselves. The woman did most of the talking. Her name was Terry. She said she had heard about Tommy's injury at a meeting hosted by WorkMatters, a Christian ministry run by our friend David Roth. After the meeting, as Terry was praying for Tommy, she said God had told her Tommy would walk again. When this occurred, she said, Tommy would walk in and testify about God's healing power to a large group of people.

She read Psalm 46 and then explained that her son had been paralyzed in an accident at age seventeen, had lived five years before dying, and that she had written a book about their story. She said God had told her this wonderful news about Tommy, and she felt compelled to share it.

We were encouraged to hear it, of course, but I couldn't help but wonder about her credibility. Why was I skeptical about her when I knew God could and did sometimes perform such miracles? After all, we *were* praying daily for a complete healing. Was God promising this to us?

Not long after this stranger came to see Tommy and Robyn, an older friend of Robyn's from church named Harriet approached her to tell her virtually the same thing. In fact, Harriet wrote Tommy and Robyn a letter in which she talked about the Holy Spirit "turning on a switch" inside Tommy's spine to heal him. Robyn knew her to be a person in touch with the Holy Spirit.

It wasn't until weeks later, at dinner together in Denver while Tommy was in rehab, that Robyn told me about Harriet's "prophecy." Robyn told me almost in a whisper and said it was "just between us" for right now. She told me she didn't know what to do other than accept it as God's message to us. The way Robyn said it, I took it to mean that while she believed in Tommy's healing, these prophecies of recovery seemed crazy in the face of so many negative medical reports.

By then we knew Tommy's injury had moved all the way up to "C zero," which is above the first vertebra at the base of the brain. This meant that medically a case could be easily made that the odds were very high that Tommy would never be off the ventilator, much less be able to use any of his limbs or walk again.

But Robyn's faith was very strong, and, like Vicki and

me, she believed in miracles. She lived every day with that hope and with the belief that God is good and that He has a beautiful plan for us. Her ability to block out the horrible "what if" prognosis of the future was amazing to me. She focused on the "right now, today" and sought God's help daily as well as anyone I have ever seen.

DALLAS OR DENVER

Tommy was finally able to have the tracheotomy on Thursday, February 26. After that, it was time to move him to a rehabilitation hospital as soon as possible.

I reflect on Tommy's time at Washington Regional Medical Center with a thankfulness for the team there. Dr. Knox and Dr. Brooks were indeed very competent and communicative. And the staff responded with grace and professionalism to our "high maintenance" family. One of us was almost always with Tommy except late at night, and we called often for attention. But nurses like Stephanie and Brandi were like angels hovering over Tommy, trying to make him comfortable.

We did have one grouchy and negative nurse whom I dubbed "the Knuckle Cracker" (to our family only). Robyn, Tommy, and I began praying for her, and we noticed she became more attentive and positive. Robyn told me later that Tommy had told the cranky nurse that he loved her by silently moving his lips.

While we appreciated everyone at Washington Regional, it doesn't operate as a rehab hospital, so it's rare for patients like Tommy to stay there for very long. And we were concerned that the delays leading up to both surgeries might somehow have jeopardized Tommy's long-term recovery.

We had been planning for three weeks to send Tommy

to Baylor University Medical Center in Dallas. We knew
Baylor had a good reputation for care for this type of injury.
And Tommy and Robyn had lived in Dallas for fifteen years
before moving to Fayetteville, so they had an extensive
network of friends and family there, including Robyn's
sister, Brenda, and brother, Doug. Several of those friends
offered to help the family, including one who promised a
free place for Robyn to live.

But on the evening after the tracheotomy, Dr. Brooks
received an odd call from one of the doctors at Baylor.
Someone at Baylor was questioning whether Tommy
was a good fit for their patient mix since he was still on
a ventilator. They claimed they thought he would be off
of it before he was transferred to Baylor. This was a very
perplexing statement; we never had any idea he would be
off the ventilator at this juncture of his recovery. Dr. Brooks
became very upset, and the call left the whole family in
turmoil as to where Tommy should go to rehab.

This infuriated me because we were under pressure to
get Tommy to rehab *immediately*. I questioned why, after
three long weeks of planning for a major move to Baylor,
this question was just now coming up. I was praying about
this frustration on Friday morning while driving back
from a business retreat, when suddenly it occurred to me
that maybe the Lord was telling us to look at alternative
hospitals. My prayer changed on the spot, and I began to
pray for guidance about what to do next.

Over the next weekend, the whole family prayed about
this decision. In the meantime, we began hearing positive
comments from several directions about Craig Hospital
in Denver. Dr. Brooks had sent other rehab patients to
Craig with good results. He contacted Craig that weekend,
and they immediately arranged to fly a representative to

Fayetteville on that Monday to evaluate Tommy's condition and to meet the family. After Baylor's hesitancy, this proactive interest was refreshing.

In addition, I called my close friend Dr. Barry Baskin, a rehab doctor in Little Rock, to ask his opinion. Barry in turn called his friend, a professor of physical medicine at the University of Arkansas for Medical Sciences who specializes in the spine, to ask his opinion. The report back was that Craig Hospital was one of the country's finest regional treatment centers.

During that same conversation, Barry told me that another friend, Dr. Al Alexander, a radiologist, had read Tommy's MRI. He concurred that the injury was higher than the C5 vertebra, at least up to the C2 vertebra. This part of the spinal cord controls breathing, so it was very much in question whether or not Tommy would ever get off the ventilator.

This news was very hard for me to hear, but it doubled my resolve to make sure Tommy was in the very best rehab hospital. It appeared to me that Craig was it; however, the decision was Tommy and Robyn's to make. The previous momentum was strong to go to Baylor if they would accept him.

Robyn and Vicki pulled up the web pages for both Craig and Baylor to compare the two and to share with Tommy. Craig was impressive, but Tommy favored the security of being with friends in Dallas. My concern, meanwhile, turned to whether we could get Tommy into Craig in any timely manner, even if we all agreed he should go there.

A QUICK DECISION

Family support was one of three criteria for acceptance to Craig, so it was no surprise that Suzanne Riccio, the representative from Craig, wanted to meet with us when she arrived that Monday in Fayetteville.

Robyn, Mud, Marshall, Beth, Vicki, and I all arrived promptly at 7:30 a.m. and waited while she met with Tommy and began reviewing his medical records.

She was very gracious and warm when she met with the family, but also clinical and matter-of-fact. She quickly got to the point: Tommy appeared to have a C2 injury, which wasn't a surprise to me after Barry had said the same just the day before. This was devastating to the rest of our family, however, since others had not heard it before now.

At that juncture, I stopped her to say that we were happy to spend a half day with her assessing the situation, but we needed to know if we had a legitimate shot to get Tommy into Craig Hospital if he chose to go there. Our prayer all weekend was that God would guide us, and I felt we needed to know if Tommy would be accepted before we invested too much emotional energy with her. We were already emotionally fragile, and at that point we didn't need any more reversals.

Within two hours, they offered to accept Tommy by Wednesday—only two days away. Since Craig Hospital was almost always full with long-term patients, she said, an opportunity to be admitted there so quickly was "quite unusual." It seemed the decision was clear. God had redirected us to look at Craig, and now He had opened its doors to us. So, Tommy and Robyn flew by air ambulance to Denver on Thursday, March 5, Robyn's forty-sixth birthday.

REFLECTIONS: SEVEN YEARS LATER

By Robyn Van Zandt

I firmly believe God's grace was in me and His protection surrounded me during the first few weeks following Tommy's accident. It was like I was entering into a completely new world, but at the same time trying to stay connected to my old world—my children and my friends.

For me, God's grace manifested itself in this physical warmth that was pretty constant for about two weeks. I was very aware of God's presence during this time, and some people commented that I literally glowed. I was not at all aware of that, but I did feel it inside. There were times when I walked through the hospital and felt as if I were floating.

It sounds so weird, and it was surreal. I wondered if other people have felt that or if maybe I made it up.

Since then, I had a conversation with a friend who had recently been confronted with news that her husband was diagnosed with cancer. She expressed a similar feeling. For two weeks, she was keenly aware of God's presence. She expressed something else I was feeling—an overwhelming gratitude for the love coming from the people who surrounded us. It is so big that it is hard to wrap your head around how to receive or respond to it. I think that's just amazing, because the shock is just so overwhelming.

Another way I think God saw me through those first weeks was through prophecies from other people who told us Tommy would be healed.

I am always willing to believe, but I know discernment is also important. It's hard to be skeptical, however, when you are desperate for some hope for physical healing.

At that time, it was good and encouraging to have that hope, because I didn't have the fortune of being able to see all the blessings I've seen in the years since Tommy's accident. I needed hope until I could get to the point where I could see and appreciate the blessings that come from other possibilities.

Now, I can accept it if it's not God's will to physically heal Tommy on earth. Of course, there's still a part of me that says, "You never know! You just never know!" I'm always open to that possibility.

Chapter 3

Big Challenges

*Now faith is confidence in what we hope for
and assurance about what we do not see.*
HEBREWS 11:1 (NIV)

Moving Tommy eight hundred miles from his home brought unique challenges.

For starters, we had to hire an air ambulance on short notice to take Tommy and Robyn to Denver. Doug Sims, Robyn's brother and a radiologist in Dallas, immediately offered to pay the cost ($10,500) since Tommy's insurance didn't cover it. This was a huge help.

We also had to think through practical issues, like how to care for Ross (seventeen years old) and Jack (fourteen years old) while their mother was with their dad in Denver. And we had to evaluate and address the tremendous financial strain the tragedy was having on Tommy's family. He had, at least temporarily, lost his job just as the economy was going into a deep recession. The normal bills weren't going away, and the medical expenses were mounting.

But the biggest adjustment for the family during Tommy's first month in Denver was emotional. We all had to figure out how best to deal with this recently "flipped" world.

I flew to Denver a couple of days behind Tommy and Robyn with the goal of helping them settle in for the long rehab period at the hospital. But I also wanted to bring back reassurance to the family at home that everything was going well. One of the first things I did was send photos of Tommy, Tommy's room, the sky bridge to the hospital, and Robyn's temporary apartment. For Mud's benefit, we even took pictures of Robyn's cabinets and refrigerator, because Mud worried about whether there was enough for her to eat in Denver.

While I was there, Dr. John James dropped in for a visit. John lives in the Denver area and is an old friend and fraternity brother of Tommy's. He had been injured about three years previously when the driver of a car ran over him on his bicycle, and he had been treated over many months right there at Craig Hospital.

John described the extent of his injuries to us, including internal organ damage that required multiple surgeries. He learned how to walk again at Craig after many months of rehabilitation. And he told us how strange he felt to be back at the hospital for the first time since being dismissed. Recollections of the pain, and also the kind treatment he received there, all came rushing back to him as he limped in to see us. It's hard to overstate how inspirational it was for Tommy, Robyn, and me to see John. He was a living example of grit and determination. And he had recovered, a hope that we needed desperately to see.

John, Robyn, and I rolled Tommy out to the sky bridge at the hospital so Tommy could get a view of Pikes Peak. It was the first time in more than a month—the first time since the injury—that Tommy had been exposed to direct sunlight.

My trip lasted only a couple of days, but Robyn and I took time during the trip to have lunch alone. We walked to a restaurant a block or two from the hospital on a beautiful, cool, sunny day. We talked about family and my travel plans to go home, but nothing heavy. It was a real treat for us, because it was the first time since the accident that we could visit when we were not in a hospital or in a traumatic situation at their home.

She would stay in Denver with Tommy for several more weeks to help him get used to his new environment and to get to know the caregivers who would help him, while I returned to help with the rest of the family in Arkansas.

My Journal, March 15, 2009

I read the first chapter of Luke during my morning devotional time. The Virgin Mary, as a very young woman, was visited by the angel Gabriel, who told her she would give birth to God's Son, Jesus. Although she asked how this could happen since she was a virgin, she immediately accepted that God could perform this miracle and responded, "I am the Lord's servant. May everything you have said about me come true" (verse 38, NLT).

Soon after, Mary visited Elizabeth (pregnant with John the Baptist at her very old age). Elizabeth told her, "You are blessed because you believed that the Lord would do what he said" (verse 45, NLT).

When I read those verses, I felt guilty that I had not been able to believe the prophecies about Tommy's recovery. I needed to let go of "how" or "why" this recovery could happen and instead have faith that the Lord could be speaking through these people to us. I was finally able to accept the possibility in an emotional time alone today.

Vicki and I had a long talk about these feelings. She had felt all along that God would heal Tommy and that we had to be optimistic and continually pray for "complete recovery." On this day, I was finally able to cross the line of faith and to expect that recovery.

MAPPING THE FINANCES

Tommy had always handled his family's finances, and Robyn had no emotional capacity to take on the challenge of understanding them after the accident. So, with help from our team at Sage Partners, I took on the task. I gathered the bills as they came to the house, brought them to the office, and created a family financial picture with the help of one of our administrative assistants.

There were regular bills—water, electricity, two mortgages, credit cards, etc.—and then there were the medical bills that insurance didn't cover, starting with the $6,000 deductible. Plus, there were looming expenses related to Tommy's long-term care. So we needed to map a plan for the present and the future.

Before his big surgery, Tommy agreed to a living will and a government HIPPA release allowing us access to his medical records. He also granted power of attorney to Robyn, me, and Brian Shaw (our friend and business partner). It was hard to stand in Tommy's ICU room at Washington Regional as he lay there blinking "yes" for approval of these documents. However, they proved invaluable in the coming weeks when we performed the mundane financial tasks like paying bills and filing insurance claims.

As I gathered other financial information, such as loan balances, house mortgage information, and life and disability policy details, it soon was very clear that a major financial challenge lay ahead. Tommy had a good income before the accident, but he had no way to work in its immediate aftermath. Even in the best of times, this would have proved difficult. And these weren't normal times. The "great recession" that began in late 2008 was in full swing at the time of the accident. The stock market had dropped some 40 percent in 2008, and about 20 percent the first two weeks of 2009.

Tommy had invested with several of us in a handful of real estate properties in the Northwest Arkansas area over the previous few years. Unfortunately, most were raw land for development. He used profits from previous investments to fund these transactions. But the prospects for developing these sites began to dwindle as the overall economy began to soften. So, he had to use ordinary income to pay back loans, and one of the major income-producing tenants stopped paying rent.

In February, Sage had zero revenue for the first time in its four-year history. Zero revenue to Sage meant zero revenue to all of its producers, including Tommy. Furthermore, payments from Tommy's private disability policy ($2,000 per month) wouldn't come in until the third month after the accident. And payments from his government Social Security/disability (estimated at $2,000 to $3,000 per month) wouldn't arrive until the sixth month after the accident. The house payments (first and second mortgages) totaled $3,700. At this time, there were no savings other than a 401k and cash balances in life insurance accounts.

The more I learned, the more I realized bankruptcy was a frighteningly real possibility for the Van Zandt family. And I began to prepare mentally for the potentially huge expenses that Vicki and I might need to incur to care for Tommy over the long run. My fear was that over the long haul, the expenses could wipe us out financially as well. About this time, we took out a mortgage on our home after having proudly paid it off several years earlier. With all our additional expenses, and very little income during those months, we needed some extra money.

I remember feeling quite overwhelmed—and probably a little sorry for myself—the first time I met with Tommy's banker. After she laid out the details of his loans and collateral, she asked how Tommy was doing and then very confidently declared that she felt he would be fine. She almost seemed a little calloused as she said it, but then she opened up a little to tell me her own story of family struggle. It involved an unplanned pregnancy for a baby to be born only eleven months after her first child. At first, she and her husband were worried they couldn't afford a second child. Later they were told that the second child would have spina bifida and likely was brain damaged, as well.

She had seven days to decide whether to abort the baby. Only after deciding not to have the abortion, when there was no turning back, did she learn the baby was not brain damaged. She showed me pictures of her two beautiful children. Several weeks later, I saw them at church. The little boy needed a walker to get around, but otherwise seemed perfectly normal.

I remember leaving the meeting in admiration of the banker, while also deciding I had better toughen up because lots of people dealt with trauma every day.

The Family Trust

As the financial picture became clear, I became increasingly distressed about it. Yet Tommy was in such critical condition that I couldn't bear to bring it up to Robyn or Vicki. Both were using every bit of energy trying to be positive with Tommy, the family, and the community.

I turned to my old friend Ron Clark for advice.

Ron is not only one of my closest friends but also is a brilliant, level-headed thinker. He is a former managing partner of the Rose Law Firm, and he was our family attorney until he took the job as general counsel with The Stephens Group. He quickly grasped the details of the financial picture and immediately pressed me to create a trust to help the family. At the same time, Tommy's good friend (and mine from Fort Smith days) Tony Sherman also urged me to create such a fund.

After talking generally about our need, Robyn and Vicki agreed to move forward with it. Ron worked over a weekend on his own time and at no charge to draft the trust. He also asked Brian Rosenthal, his friend at the Rose Law Firm, to help us stave off the credit card debt. Brian also volunteered to help at no charge.

We felt it was important to announce the creation of a trust on the blog as quickly as possible since so many people followed it daily. I drafted a simple paragraph that explained the need for and the purpose of the trust. When I ran it by Ron, he tactfully told me it was not strong enough to convey the depth of the need. Then he drafted a suggested paragraph, which we used verbatim and which still has a spot on the blog's home page.

Checks immediately started rolling in from all over the country, and it quickly became apparent that Tommy had touched people all of his life.

One check came in from Dallas with a note that said Tommy was one of the first people she had met in the real estate business twenty years earlier. Another came from Betty Adkins, Tommy's respiratory therapist in the Fayetteville ICU. Each check represented a story of love and a history of a relationship to someone in the family. And each check was an encouragement.

TEAM MEETING 1.0

On Monday, March 16, Robyn and Tommy asked me to participate in a "team meeting" via conference call with the medical team in Denver. The team consisted of Tommy's doctor (Dr. Johansen), the head nurse, his occupational therapist, his physical therapist, his psychologist, and a family services representative. They were all in Tommy's room with him and Robyn. Dr. Wayne Brooks and Robyn's brother also dialed in.

During the call, each team member reported their view of Tommy's condition and also the next steps for their area of focus. It was an impressive display of knowledge and communication. Dr. Johansen even presented Tommy's latest MRI (taken that morning) to those in the room and analyzed what he was seeing.

The picture was not pretty. The MRI showed spinal cord damage all the way to C zero, the base of the brain. Some nerves looked healthy, some damaged, and others uncertain. The injury was classified as "A" on a scale of A through E, with A being the most severe. It was clear that any mobility in the future was uncertain.

Yet Dr. Johansen reiterated a case for hope. We needed something to "turn the switch on" in Tommy's spine, he said, so the nerves would somehow reroute.

Robyn was amazed. This was the very term used by her

friend Helen in the letter to Tommy written many weeks earlier. Helen had said she was praying for the Holy Spirit to "turn the switch on" in Tommy's body so he could heal. And she said she thought Tommy would walk again, just as the woman named Terry had announced weeks ago in the ICU at Washington Regional.

The team call also confirmed what we knew—that Tommy had numerous medical issues standing in the way of rehab. He had a skin laceration on his rear end that prevented him from sitting upright. This probably was a result of being in bed for weeks, unable to turn himself. Now he had to be constantly rolled over in bed on his right or his left side for weeks to allow this condition to heal.

Tommy was anemic, so he had needed blood transfusions both in Fayetteville and now in Denver. His blood sugar was high. His body "thermostat" was not working, so he was either hot or cold much of the time. His teeth ached, likely from nerve damage. From the beginning, Tommy had a lot of fluid in his lungs, which required frequent suctioning and antibiotics to treat.

Obviously, Tommy was still a very sick man, even five weeks after the injury.

After the team call, Robyn called me and broke down emotionally. Fortunately, I was strong at that moment, so I could support her. At other times, I broke down myself, but not in front of her.

As always, Robyn was only down for a few minutes. After a short time of quiet sobbing, she would always come back to the same points: "God is good. God has a plan in all of this. Look what He is doing to impact all of these people and to help us. God is telling us that Tommy is going to get well. This will all pass. God will help us. Isn't He sweet to show us all of these plans? Let's focus on today."

And then we moved on. What an incredible person. What faith! She was an inspiration to me.

MAKING ADJUSTMENTS

Robyn worked hard to help Tommy stay positive while in Denver. For instance, she handwrote a small sign that she placed on the bookshelf in the hospital room so Tommy could see it when he was turned on that side in bed. It said, "Now faith is confidence in what we hope for and assurance about what we do not see" (Hebrews 11:1).

Not only did this help Tommy, but it also led to discussions later between Tommy and visitors and staff who came in and out of his room.

Other members of our immediate family were awesome during this time, as well. Each person reacted differently based on the various personalities.

Tommy's mother, Mud, was very strong. She did best around family, but sometimes she was lonesome by herself at home. She told me at times she felt "far removed" from Tommy, with him and Robyn in Denver and their sons with us in Fayetteville three hours away.

Mud is incredibly devoted to her family. She displayed this most vividly with her nurturing and commitment to Big Dad after a stroke left him paralyzed on his right side. She nursed him at home for twelve years until she couldn't physically do it any more, then visited him almost every day, usually multiple times, when he was in the nursing home the last three years of his life.

Mud shared with me that she had been reading Mark 4:30–32 about faith being like a mustard seed, and that it had given her great comfort since Tommy's injury.

Vicki responded to this tragedy with her typical "take charge" attitude. She immediately recognized that Ross and Jack needed consistency in their lives so they could stay in school and sleep in their own beds throughout Tommy's long recovery process. She felt strongly that we should move to Fayetteville right away to provide that consistency.

She found a college student, Bess Jones, to move into our house in Little Rock and to take care of our beloved Labrador retriever, Dixie. After raising two sons of our own, Vicki was right back to fixing sack lunches for school, driving football practice carpool, and checking grades. She was good at it the first time, and she hadn't forgotten a thing. I joked that fourteen-year-old Jack had never had such an eagle eye on him.

Vicki has a strong faith. She did not need nor want to hear too many negative details about Tommy's medical condition. She stayed focused on a firm belief that he was going to get well.

And she kept very busy taking care of the boys. Once I noticed her polishing the same spot on the kitchen counter for what seemed like thirty minutes after dinner. My assumption was that she was deep in thought. Moving just helped her process what was happening.

Ross had always been mature for his age. At seventeen, he was now thrust into a position of maturing much beyond his years. On the very Saturday that Tommy was injured, friends at Central United Methodist Church hastily called for a prayer service. Ross stood up in front of the whole chapel full of people and gave a faith testimony, declaring that he knew his dad would get well.

Five weeks later, while on a Spring Break mission trip to Mexico, he sent this text to Robyn:

Hey mom, I'm just checking in with you. I'm having a blast! I have been doing a lot of demo/construction and outreaches lately. Today I went to a poor neighborhood with a woman and prayed for a boy who is dying because he got run over by a car. Many other interesting things have happened that I can't wait to tell you about.

How is Dad? I'm sure he is great. All of the disabled children here are the happiest at the orphanage ... that has been a great witness to me because I think God is trying to show me that even if Dad has disabilities he can still enjoy life to the fullest. I love you and Dad!!!!! Can't wait to see y'all next week.

Jack, fourteen at the time, struggled initially to express his anxiety about his dad. He spent a lot of time on Facebook or texting friends, and we spent a lot of time shuttling him to and from the mall or movies so he could see the friends he had been texting all day long.

One day over a hamburger, he finally told me, "If this was going to happen to Dad, I wish it had happened later." He was processing the fact that he would not have the same experiences as a teenager that Ross had with his dad.

When he "talked out" in English class (for the second time) and a note of reprimand was sent home to Robyn (now surrogate mother Vicki), Jack said it wasn't his fault and that everyone talked in that class. He claimed the teacher was being unfair by singling him out. Vicki calmly volunteered to go to the school and monitor that class to ensure the teacher was being fair. Of course, it was Jack's worst nightmare to have his aunt show up and embarrass him in front of all of his eighth-grade friends. The talking in class stopped. He had met his match in Vicki!

Our sons, Marshall and John Mark, along with Marshall's wife, Beth, and John Mark's girlfriend, Melissa, were very helpful. Marshall and Beth focused on helping with Jack and Ross in Fayetteville, while John Mark and Melissa checked on Mud since they were in Little Rock with her.

Our sons dearly love Tommy. We have always been a close family, together each year on the long Thanksgiving weekend and seeing each other quite a bit year-round. The kids have great memories of camping in Lake Ouachita together on Memorial Day weekends. Tommy has taken Ross and Jack duck hunting or fishing with us many times, and now Marshall works with Tommy at Sage Partners. With these deep relationships, their desire to help in any way was heartfelt. The impact on them was profound, and I could see it clearly.

I saw Tommy's accident as having an especially major impact on Marshall. He and I, independent of each other, had taken *The Shack* by William Paul Young to read while in Argentina. The book is about a man's tragic loss of his daughter and his subsequent bitterness toward God. It ends with reconciliation and a new personal relationship between God and the man. I had started the book on the plane ride south, but I put it down during the part about the daughter's murder.

Who needs to read this while on vacation? I thought.

Marshall had continued to read it and finished the book on the trip. He told me the book had been a "life-changer" and that it basically provided beautiful insight into the depth of God's love for someone who has gone through an unthinkable tragedy.

My sister, Ann, told me her son, Andrew Appleton, was asking her how something like this tragedy could happen to somebody as good as Tommy. When I told Marshall about Andrew's struggle, he told me to recommend the book to him, which I did.

I didn't view the timing of Marshall's reading of *The*

Shack (and my own) as coincidence, but as God reaching out to us to help us deal with Tommy's accident.

MY TRAUMA

The trauma we were going through had a bigger impact on me than I would have expected. I love Tommy like a younger brother. Tommy had always looked up to me, because he looked up to Vicki, his only sibling. Tommy once told me he had always wanted to be my business partner, and it had become a reality at Sage.

Now it pained me deeply to see him suffer like this. I went through periodic breakdowns and would weep quietly to myself when alone, trying to be strong in front of him and the rest of the family. This was very strange for me, because for twenty-five years in my early manhood, nothing made me cry, ever. Nothing had affected me in my life to this extent except for the illness of my own beautiful mother, who fought breast cancer for nine years. The difference was that Tommy's tragedy was so immediate and so intense.

REFLECTIONS: SEVEN YEARS LATER

By Tommy Van Zandt

After it was clear that I had survived the initial fall from the ladder, I never had the thought that I was going to die. They kept all the stress, all the worry, a lot of the medical stuff—the life-or-death things—away from me. I didn't find out for a few years some of the things, like that it was a miracle I made it to the hospital at all. Most people with that injury lose their breath.

They insulated me from so much. They wanted me to rest and relax. They wanted me to have peace. I was five foot ten and weighed 155 pounds. I was lean. I exercised and tried to eat right. And I had ADD before they knew what it was. I was running around going all the time.

So for a guy like me with my personality to be paralyzed and not be able to go and take care of things, that would have made me very depressed and anxious and scared. God's grace was with me and still is. I just have a sense of peace about me that I'm going to be OK and my fate is in God's hands.

God doesn't cause bad things to happen, but God's there to pick you up when bad things do happen. So I had this peace about me, and I still do.

I don't remember anything about the surgery,

except that I couldn't talk. They kept saying they would fix that, that it was only temporary. Communication. That was the first frustration. I was blinking "yes" or "no" in the very beginning. Then some friends made a board with letters on it. So to answer in one word, like *hungry,* I'd have to go through the board and when they'd hit the right letter, I'd blink.

Once I got the ability to talk again, I wanted to know where my phone was. I was thinking about work and deals. I wanted to read e-mails. My connection to the outside world was my phone. I remember when BlackBerry first allowed for e-mail … *Oh, my gosh,* I thought, *I can do this from anywhere, 24/7!* I was pretty attached to it. And work was heavy on my mind.

Somebody would have to push the button for me to then speak into the Bluetooth and request to call someone. Then they would turn it off.

I had a lot of time alone, so I wanted to know what was going on with my business and with my friends. It was a big deal, because at that point I was finally able to speak in an audible fashion. I was healing more overall. I was more aware of what I was missing. My thoughts were going to the outside versus within my own head and hospital room.

Chapter 4

Unusual Events in Denver

I can do all things through Christ who strengthens me.
PHILIPPIANS 4:13 (NKJV)

On Wednesday, March 25, our friends Neal and Gina Pendergraft took Jack and Ross to Denver to see their dad at Craig Hospital for the first time. The Pendergrafts had been supportive of the family from the first day of the injury, and this was just one of many examples of how they helped.

It turned out to be a challenging trip for the boys, but not because of their father's condition.

The day after they arrived, Ross called around noon to say his mother was not doing well and that she felt someone else needed to come to Denver to help Tommy until she felt better. I realized we had all been so focused on Tommy that we had not worried about Robyn. The stress had begun to take a serious toll on her physical health.

She often felt faint, Ross said, and she would need to sit down unexpectedly. Then she would begin shaking uncontrollably. Thankfully, Ross was mature beyond his years. He and I spoke several times that afternoon, and I never felt like I was dealing with an overwhelmed teenager. And when Robyn's condition got worse, Ross stayed calm and called 911 for an ambulance to come get his mom.

The ambulance was dispatched from Swedish Medical Center, which is right next to Craig Hospital. Getting her across the street was more difficult than you might imagine, however, because all of this occurred while a blizzard hit the city.

The whole situation seemed surreal to me. We had an ambulance coming next door to a rehab hospital to pick up the caregiver who had been so strong for so long. I was horrified over this scene and the fact that Ross had to orchestrate it all.

As Ross and Jack watched them load their mother into an ambulance while in the midst of a blizzard, I asked Ross if they were OK. He told me they were fine, but that they were hungry. Finally, he was acting like a teenager!

Once Robyn made it to the emergency room at Swedish Medical Center, the doctors ran several tests to ascertain her condition. The most obvious problem was that her blood pressure had shot up to 175. They gave her fluids for dehydration and released her later that evening after her blood pressure came down.

In conversations with her that night and the next day, Vicki and I could hear that she was at the end of her emotional rope. We made quick plans for me to fly to Denver that Sunday to be with Tommy so Robyn could fly home with the boys that same night. Vicki drove back to Fayetteville, meanwhile, to greet them. She would have to take care of the boys and Robyn.

Beyond Blinking

My second trip to spend time with Tommy in Denver was dramatically different from the first. For starters, Tommy didn't even remember that I had been there for two days only a couple of weeks before. He knew that my trip was unscheduled due to Robyn's illness, and he also knew that Robyn was feeling better by the time I arrived.

More importantly, Tommy now was able to have real conversations. They had fitted Tommy's "trach" with a cuff, which allowed him to talk while still on the ventilator.

It almost felt like a loved one who had died had come back to life. After all of the time standing over his bedside, his mouth taped shut, it was a huge relief just to hear him express his thoughts. After weeks of communicating by blinking, now he could talk. And if there's one thing Tommy likes to do, it's talk!

"First of all, you don't need to be here," he told me shortly after I arrived. "I am doing much better, and the staff here is great. You have too much to do to stay here with me."

This was awesome. Tommy was trying to take charge, being bossy.

That first conversation lasted three hours, interrupted by the almost constant stream of caregivers. He told me he was "kicking butt now." He was optimistic, and he was ready to fight. He told me how his boys had taken care of him all weekend. He especially bragged on Jack, describing how attentive and helpful he had been. We also talked about a few real estate deals and his concerns about their family financial picture. Mostly, he talked about the many people who had touched him.

Finally, late in this conversation, I felt compelled to ask Tommy the question that had been on my mind for many weeks: "Tommy," I said, "how did you fall?"

He explained that he was using a chain saw to cut a heavy limb off a big tree in his backyard. When the limb was partially cut, the end of it swung down hard and knocked the ladder he was standing on out from under him. It happened so fast that Tommy's thought was to throw the chain saw away from him, but he flipped in the process, landing on his head.

I stared at him in silence for a moment. Anger welled up inside of me. I knew the tree he was describing. To me, in pre-spring March, it was barren and ugly anyway. And now I hated it. I hated it for what had happened under it to Tommy and to our whole family. I hated it for what it represented. And in my mind, none of us should have to look at it ever again.

"Tommy, will you let me cut down that damned tree?" I said.

Now, Tommy stared at me for a moment.

"Not right now," he said.

I accepted his answer, even though I didn't like it. Perhaps he would think about it some more and relent later. I never brought it up again and Tommy didn't, either. Looking back, I know Tommy never intended to have it cut down. He recognized the beauty of that tree from better times. He had seen it during beautiful sunrises and sunsets, leafed out in full glory. Perhaps those memories symbolized that better times were coming, for him and the tree.

My Journal, March 10, 2009

We've seen some amazing events happen in individual people's lives because of Tommy's situation.

Today, for instance, a friend whom I had not

seen in years came into my office. He was one of the family friends who inspired me as a young man to go into the real estate industry. He asked all about Tommy, and I could see the sorrow on his face as I described Tommy's condition. I told him how the Lord had helped us to get Tommy into Craig Hospital and that we felt confident Tommy should be there because of God's direction in getting it done.

The conversation shifted, and he began telling me about the challenges he faced with the various real estate developments he's involved in around the country. He is feeling the brunt of the recession and the horrid banking environment. He's been very successful for more than forty years. I'm guessing he's earned tens of millions of dollars during that time. Now he faces the possibility of losing everything.

But he told me that something was bothering him more than losing money. He said he regretted many of his actions and was fearful that God would never forgive him. He specifically said he was worried about eternity because he felt he had not done what God had asked him to do with his life. Then he quoted a Scripture he had seen on Tommy's blog that he had later looked up in his Bible.

I nearly fell out of my chair. It was a very personal confession, one I never expected to hear from him. We had never discussed much of anything but business, and then only very infrequently. Tommy's injury, and the Scripture on the blog, had clearly had a major impact on this man's life. I closed the meeting by telling him that if Christ could forgive two criminals on the cross next to Him

on the day of their death, then Christ would surely
forgive him. He merely needed to accept Christ's
grace. I didn't know what else to say.

Sufficient Grace

Many of Tommy's medical complications (distended
ilium, high insulin levels, out-of-whack blood count) had
improved, but plenty remained. We were mainly praying
for relief from the pain in his teeth and head, and also for
the skin on his rear end to heal.

The skin complication was holding back his rehab
progress because it kept him from sitting upright. It was
not getting worse, but it also was not getting better.

The sharp pains that sometimes evolved into a severe
headache at the top of his head were very hard on him. He
became emotional as he described that at the peak of this
pain, he felt God was right there close to him, walking with
him.

This reminded me of 2 Corinthians 12:7–9, so we read
the passage together. It describes the apostle Paul praying
for God to take away his torment, yet God letting him
endure it, saying, "My grace is sufficient for you, for my
power is made perfect in weakness (NIV)."

Later that day, Tommy told me his pain was better than
it had been in a long time. A day earlier, the pain had been
a seven or eight on a scale of ten, he said, but now it was a
two. God had answered our prayer for help that morning.

Return of the "Crackberry"

On this same trip, the occupational rehab specialist and I
began working on a way for Tommy to make voice-activated

phone calls so he could reach out to Robyn and others to tell them he was doing OK.

Tommy had a special affinity for his phone, a BlackBerry that he used so much before the accident that we jokingly called it his "Crackberry." For a few days after the accident, while he was in a state of semi-consciousness in the Fayetteville hospital, Tommy had made Robyn lay it by him on the bed, sort of like an electronic security blanket. When I joked with Robyn about this, she became a little emotional because she knew it was one way Tommy was trying to cling to his life before the accident.

It took a couple of days, but soon we had the BlackBerry attached by Velcro to his bed. Tommy had a lifeline to the world. The occupational therapist also began to teach Tommy how to use Dragon voice recognition software so eventually he could surf the Internet or dictate e-mails. Tommy told me later that the software didn't work well for him, so we continued to seek other alternatives for him to communicate electronically.

Sweet Dreams

Tommy and I talked about other encouraging messages from our friends, including one from Eddie Drilling. Eddie had e-mailed me the prior week to share a very vivid dream he had in which Tommy was walking around. The walking was not "totally normal," he said, but Tommy was walking.

Brian Shaw, our partner and friend, had also e-mailed Robyn that day and asked her to tell Tommy about a dream he had in which he and Tommy were fishing.

"We weren't catching anything, as usual," Brian told her, "but we were fishing."

Finally, Tommy asked me to read a two-page typed letter from a man in Little Rock who had read about Tommy in the local newspaper. Neither of us knew this man, but he had written Tommy to share his story of injury, paralysis, and subsequent recovery. He offered three specific suggestions for recovery: faith, measuring progress weekly (not daily), and taking charge of your own health care. All of these encouragements helped Tommy.

DISTURBING PROSPECTS

Some days were not so encouraging; in fact, some days were troubling. One day in particular the "wound specialist" reported that the skin laceration on Tommy's rear end hadn't improved in the past week. If it didn't get better soon, the medical team would recommend surgical repair. This would mean another thirty-three days of flat-on-his-back bed rest to allow the skin to heal.

After almost seven weeks in bed, this was a disturbing prospect.

Less than an hour after hearing that news, the respiratory therapist came in, so I questioned her as to when and how they would determine if Tommy could be weaned off the ventilator. I did not understand why they had pressed Tommy to try to breathe on his own in Fayetteville, yet they weren't working with him on it in Denver.

The therapist explained that Tommy needed to pass a threshold on a test she would administer before beginning that work, and she offered to try it right away. During that test, she said Tommy registered "nothing." I tried to dismiss it in front of Tommy, but this bothered me a lot.

That night, alone in my apartment, I was really down. What if Tommy could never get off the ventilator? What if he had to spend another long period of time on his back when he was already dealing with so much muscle atrophy?

I thought of the Scripture Robyn had written in bold letters and taped on the bookshelf directly in front of Tommy: "Now faith is confidence in what we hope for and assurance about what we do not see" (Hebrews 11:1).

"Where was my faith?" I asked myself that day.

STRENGTHENED BY THE WORD

The next morning the Lord and I had a long meeting in my daily devotional time. I read over my bundle of Scripture memory cards, and then I read part of Philippians. The Lord strengthened me, and brightened my outlook, so I decided to share the Scriptures with Tommy.

The first two were about God hearing and answering prayers: 1 John 5:13–15 and Matthew 7:7–8. Next, we discussed John 9:3. The context of the passage is that Christ is answering a question about why a man was born blind.

"Neither this man nor his parents sinned," said Jesus, "but this happened so that the works of God might be displayed in him (NIV)."

We had a good discussion about how God was using the accident to display His presence in Tommy's life. Tommy had a unique opportunity to have his own ministry to the hundreds of people who were following his progress.

Tommy had already given a lot of thought to this. In fact, he said he and his old friend David Montgomery had been able to have their first spiritual discussion when David had visited a few weeks earlier. They had never had such a discussion, even though they had enjoyed many years of family trips together.

We ended our devotional time by reading Philippians 4:12–13. Both of us felt refreshed and strengthened, and the day continued to get better.

We had a much more positive meeting with Courtney Long, the "head nurse" as we called her. She hadn't come by much the previous two days, and Tommy had missed her. My guess is that she missed Tommy, too, since she came in toward the end of the day, plopped down in a chair, and stayed forty-five minutes while we fired question after question at her.

While she was there, a doctor and two other nurses joined us. Tommy described sensations he was having to go to the bathroom on certain days, and asked if this could be the beginning of some feeling coming back to him. He also pressed for more information about the condition of his skin laceration. Courtney said she thought it was getting better.

I asked if Tommy could have more physical therapy to address muscle atrophy, and also about any medical research projects that might be relevant to his condition. Courtney and the team very patiently answered all of our questions. Courtney emphasized that Tommy was just now getting over several of the complications caused by severe "spinal shock" and that the spinal cord was the slowest of all of the major organs to heal. This made us feel better.

Finally, she bragged on Tommy's ability to talk clearly and strongly throughout the "puffs" of the ventilator. When I asked her why, she said it was because Tommy was "stubborn." This would bode well for him in all of the challenges of his recovery.

TEARS

As I picked up my stuff in Tommy's room to go home to Little Rock, Tommy asked me to join him in prayer. He told me to put a hand on him, so I put it on his head because he could feel it there. Then he took over.

He prayed a long prayer of thanks for all of the blessings God had given him, especially for his family and friends who were helping him. He went on to thank God for helping him in the hospital and told God that he knew that He was on our side.

That moment was the only time I was glad Tommy had no feeling on his bare arm; he couldn't feel my tears rolling off onto it.

After the prayer, Tommy thanked me for coming and for everything Vicki and I were doing to help his family. Then he told me to tell Robyn not to worry about him. He was fine, he said, and not at all scared to be alone for a few days while she rested. He emphasized he had the faith and the fight to get well. He said he would "climb back to the top." And he told me (again) he was "kicking butt and taking names" from here on out.

PASSING THE TORCH

It was hard for me to go home, but I knew Tommy was well cared for by the staff at the hospital and that he was about to receive a steady stream of visitors.

Our friend Paul James, another fraternity brother, had spent an enormous amount of time contacting some of Tommy's closest friends and scheduling a series of weekend visits. So right after I left, Pat Carrigan arrived. Tommy was excited to see him, and they had a great visit.

When Pat returned, we caught up by phone to discuss his visit. He was very excited about the BlackBerry software that he bought for Tommy's phone, because it allowed Tommy to use voice commands to receive calls. This was big progress. Pat promised to pursue the final piece—enabling Tommy to initiate calls by himself.

Pat also mentioned that Tommy had requested a

special devotional time during his visit. Pat didn't report any particular details, but he said it was a "precious time" for him. Of course, this reminded me of the conversation Tommy and I had the previous week in which we discussed his unique opportunity for ministry. Obviously, Tommy was capitalizing on his opportunity to visit with his dear friend Pat, as he had with me.

Reflections: Seven Years Later

By Robyn Van Zandt

Our situation caught up to me a few weeks into our stay at Craig when I had what can only be described as an emotional meltdown.

The stress had been mounting since the beginning, but especially since the flight from Fayetteville to Denver. We had been in Fayetteville for weeks, and Tommy was sick, sick, sick. I remember getting into the air ambulance with Tommy and having to say goodbye to my boys, not knowing what I was heading into.

Then we had the craziest plane ride ever. We hit turbulence so bad that we were jumping up and down. I can get airsick anyway, so I was grabbing my Psalm book and trying to stay calm while watching them attend to Tommy. I was thinking, *God, just help us survive this trip.*

When we got there, I knew I had to become Tommy's advocate. Normally, my personality is super trusting. I think, *That's their profession. That's what they do. I should trust them.* But I couldn't do that in this situation. I had to be more questioning.

For instance, before we left Fayetteville, a friend who is a doctor had told me they do some things differently in Denver. He mentioned that they probably would pump up Tommy's lung volumes higher than a normal person could handle. It would blow out a normal person's lungs. He wasn't sure what to make of it, but he wanted me to be aware.

So I'm thinking, *I'm not a doctor. How do I advocate for him? How do I know if something's not right? I have to make sure they're taking care of him.*

There was one instance that really about killed me. They had rigged a way for him to blow into something to call for help. I walked in one day, and he said, "Robyn, this guy came in during the night. He moved the device I blow into to signal for help out of my reach and then turned on the light and laughed and said, 'Sorry,' and left."

I got this story from him, but I didn't know who to trust with it. I had this weird sense that they would take care of their own. Here's my husband whom I've trusted for twenty-eight years. They had him on some hallucinatory drugs at the time, but he wasn't out of his mind when he said it to me. I wasn't questioning him. He was clear as day. He described what the guy looked like.

That day was the first time I met with his psychiatrist, Dr. Les Butt. I was on edge and unsure what to do, but I chose to share it with him. That was so not me, but I liked this part of me.

Dr. Butt handled it perfectly. He said, "I will make sure you have a talk with the director of nursing." And they all handled it beautifully. I went in and spoke to them. They didn't treat me like I was a crazy person. She said they had a tech who fit that description and that she would check into it.

I still don't know if it happened or if it didn't. But the point is, he was extremely helpless and I was alone. I left him at night not really knowing if he was terrified or if he was being taken care of. And I couldn't escape the trauma. The hospital has housing that family members can rent, so I'd go to my room. But everyone there was dealing with something similar, so I was surrounded by trauma.

I tried to take care of myself. I would take walks and things like that. But it was difficult coming to grips with how much life had changed while being away from my family and friends.

A month went by and the boys came to see Tommy. I was rushing around like a mad woman trying to prepare for them to come. I wanted to take care of them and still take care of Tommy. I wanted them to have fun, but I also wanted them to know what was going on.

We were in the room with Tommy, and my blood pressure shot up. So they told me to go back to the apartment and rest. There I was in my little apartment. It's snowing hard, like a blizzard. I am in my long underwear, and I had lost a lot of weight. And I thought, *I can't do it anymore.* I just broke down.

Ross called Mark, and Mark said for Ross to call an ambulance.

The hospital was just across the street, but getting me there was an adventure because of the snow. The paramedics hooked me up to an IV. I was still in my long underwear, and I had to go to the bathroom really bad because they were pumping me full of fluids. I got down on my knees and crawled, because I just couldn't stand up. I was overcome.

The Pendergrafts were there visiting us, so I flew home with them. Tommy's sister, Vicki, took care of me for a few weeks. I was scared about going back, so Jill Hollis flew back with me and then she and Mark helped me move my stuff out of the apartment. I couldn't be surrounded by all that misery and tragedy, and it didn't cost much more for me to stay at a hotel.

Chapter 5

Life in Emergency Room Mode

Suffering produces perseverance; perseverance, character; and character, hope. And hope does not put us to shame.
ROMANS 5:3–5 (NIV)

After two months, the fatigue and anxiety of our family's ordeal began to take its toll on all of us, so it seemed like the perfect time for a short trip to our trout fishing cabin in Heber Springs, Arkansas.

The cabin has always been a retreat for the family. It's perched on a hillside of a beautiful wooded lot full of tall oaks and dogwoods. There's a rocky bluff behind it, and the front yard slopes down to the Little Red River. The natural beauty of the river and nearby mountains, combined with the peace and quiet of the surroundings, make it one of the most relaxing places on earth for us.

I felt we needed time together at this special place so we could regroup and refresh, and I returned from Denver eager to go to the cabin with Vicki, Robyn, and Jack. We had talked about it for a few days, and I was excited. Then

Vicki told me Jack and Robyn had decided not to come, and she felt a need to stay with Robyn because Robyn was still so frail.

I understood this on an intellectual level, but on an emotional level, it made me angry and somewhat resentful. We could never seem to establish a travel schedule for Robyn until the last minute, leaving Vicki and me in limbo about when we could return home (or elsewhere) to recharge our batteries. I had been pushing to hit what I called "a stride we could live with" on this very long-term recovery process. But I felt like nobody was listening to me as to how to do it.

In Robyn's defense, she was totally exhausted, and it was very hard for her to plan. We all were paying a price for living in what I often referred to as "emergency room mode."

Part of that price was my precious time with Vicki. I was very concerned she would be the next victim of exhaustion. Her natural reaction to the crisis was to push herself to help Robyn and the boys, and I could see it was wearing her out. I also worried about Robyn's growing dependence on Vicki to deal with the day-to-day life of shuttling kids and other normal activities. This seemed unhealthy to me for the long term.

Looking back, I know I was wrong, because Robyn just needed more time to recover. In reality, I was probably just fighting to get some parts of my life back.

After several frictional conversations with Vicki, I tried to back off and prayed for help. I sought counsel from my friend Rainer Twiford, who was right when he told me that I could not stand between Vicki and her doing what she felt was best.

So I spent most of the weekend alone at our fishing cabin.

The time was actually good for me. On Sunday, Eddie Drilling came up to fish with me for the day. He reminded me of the Scripture in Romans 5 where we learn that suffering produces perseverance, perseverance produces character, and character produces hope. And that hope does not disappoint us. He also advised me to pray for patience, which I knew was a gift of the Holy Spirit per Galatians 5:22.

All of this helped me to get through a very difficult period. While Vicki and I certainly were not at that point, it was easy for me to see why many marriages flounder when dealing with a family tragedy. It is important for couples to make time for each other, even when an intense focus is on someone else in the family. I vowed to work on this with Vicki.

When Vicki came home that next week (April 8), we spent a lot of time together. It made me feel good to see her relax a little and catch up on her rest. By the time we went back to Fayetteville on Good Friday before Easter weekend, all of us felt better. Robyn seemed good emotionally after having been at home for almost two weeks. Between Vicki's help and that of her close friends in Fayetteville, Robyn had been strengthened by her support group. Jack and Ross also seemed good after having this time with their mom.

Another encouragement came when all of our immediate family joined us in Fayetteville for Easter weekend. John Mark drove Melissa and Mud up on Saturday. Beth had planned a fun birthday party for Vicki (April 11) and John Mark (April 14) at a Mexican place called Mojitos on Saturday night. Then we all went to church on Easter Sunday.

Robyn's mother joined us for a nice Easter lunch, as well. During lunch, Robyn called Tommy, who joined us by speaker phone to say hello. This was the first time in three months that several members of the family had actually heard his voice.

All of this was enabled by our friend Paul James, who had sacrificed his family time in Little Rock to be with Tommy in Denver on Easter. Paul was the perfect friend to be with Tommy on this weekend. He not only knew Tommy well, but he also knew the routine at Craig Hospital because his brother, Dr. John James, had been a patient there following his bicycle accident.

The next day, Paul was back in Little Rock, so he called at 8:00 a.m. to check in with me. He and Tommy had gone to church at a little chapel in the hospital, he said. Tommy wanted a shave and a gown to look nice for church. Tommy sang along in the service. And as they wheeled his bed back to his room, Tommy whistled the second verse of "Christ the Lord Is Risen Today" after Paul had whistled the first verse.

CHAINED TO SOMEONE ELSE?

One of the benefits of my being home for a change was getting to attend a Tuesday neighborhood Bible study with friends. This group began meeting more than seventeen years ago in our home, and it includes men ranging in age from the thirties to the sixties. They represent most of the major denominations or no denomination at all. We typically have fourteen to eighteen men in the group, but this year we sometimes had as many as twenty-four show up.

It had grieved me a little to miss the first two meetings of the spring study, since these men and our group meant so much to me.

This spring, we were studying Philippians. And on the first day I was able to attend, the lesson covered chapter

1, verses 12–26. Here we read about the apostle Paul's imprisonment in Rome when he was physically chained to a guard for twenty-four hours a day over a two-year period. In these verses, Paul writes about his joy in Christ even in these circumstances.

The first question in the study guide asked, "Have you ever been 'chained' to someone else in a hospital bed or somewhere else? If so, were you able to share the gospel?"

Of course, I thought immediately about Tommy. I told the men about how Tommy viewed his circumstances in Denver as his opportunity to share his faith with visiting friends and with the hospital staff there. And I told them about Tommy's prayer with me when I left the hospital in Denver, when he thanked God for helping him in the hospital and told God that he knew He was on our side.

Tommy helped teach our lesson in the Bible study that day without even being there.

GETTING ON SCHEDULE

The more I thought about everything happening in our lives, the more I knew we needed a schedule to keep things coordinated. So I spent most of a day putting one together for the whole family that covered about four months.

Maybe I was motivated because that same morning I had driven nearly four hours from Little Rock to Northwest Arkansas so I could fly to Atlanta for business, rather than driving fifteen minutes to fly out of the Little Rock airport. Why the drive? We had booked an advanced airline ticket from the wrong location because we didn't have a schedule.

We needed a schedule so we could coordinate the boys' school and early summer activities with trips to Denver or elsewhere (including business trips) for Robyn, Vicki, and me. When Robyn was in Denver, Vicki and I needed to be in Fayetteville with the boys.

I had pushed for Robyn to go to Denver every other week. If we could schedule her trips, we could fill in other visitors so Tommy was not bored or lonely. And by keeping Robyn's visits shorter in duration, she would be less exhausted when she returned to Fayetteville and better able to re-acclimate with her boys.

After quizzing everyone in the family on their schedules, Cindy Green in my office formatted it so all of us could put it on our iPhone or BlackBerry. Now it seemed we were working toward some plan for a little more "normalcy" for everyone. Hopefully this would help us hit a stride we could live with over the many months to come.

VISITS FROM FRIENDS

On April 19–20, our friend and partner Brian Shaw made his first visit to Craig. I called him on Sunday afternoon, hoping to catch him in the room with Tommy. They were together on the skywalk, and Brian put the call on speaker so Tommy could talk.

Tommy said he was feeling much better and that it was a beautiful, sunny day in Denver. I was thinking how much better it made me feel to hear his voice and especially to know he was still joyful in his heart. To me, his attitude was amazing.

When Brian returned from his trip, he told me Tommy was "inspirational" to him. He also wrote the following e-mail to Paul James so that Paul could share it with those who would visit Tommy in the coming weeks and months. It paints a great picture of who Tommy is and how he was dealing with his recovery process.

To: Paul James
Subject: FW: TVZ
Paul,

As I mentioned in my previous e-mail, I had two great days with Tommy. The expectation information you provided was valuable and seemed to hold true for my visit, as well. I arrived at Craig on Sunday around 10:15 a.m. Tommy's first words were loud and clear: "What took you so long!!!!"

As you stated from your visit, he is very much the typical Tommy, joking and carrying on with anyone who enters the room. I could tell the staff at Craig loves it and gives it right back to him. He is very engaging with them and with anyone in the room. He can tell you very detailed information about each of his caregivers, and there are quite a few. I was very impressed with the staff. They are very professional, but keep the mood very light.

On Sunday, I stayed in the room with him until around noon, when Tommy was ready for a short nap. I returned around 1:30 p.m. and stayed until 6:00 p.m. He seemed to enjoy talking about the local news and, of course, the Razorback football team. I brought along the *Democrat-Gazette* and read him the latest spring football report.

In the afternoon, it was a beautiful day and he wanted to go out on the sky bridge. It took about twenty minutes for the staff to get his bed and various accessories ready to move out of the room. He joked with them, asking if we were going to the sky bridge or to the moon, with the amount of equipment and devices we had to assemble just to make the move out of the room. We spent about forty-five minutes there, which was nice until the warmth of the room was too much for both of us.

He is still recovering from the bedsore before they will allow him to sit up or move around very much. I understood this may take a couple more weeks. However, all day long, a staff member was dropping by and paying close attention to his every need. He stays busy most of the day and really doesn't seem to have time to watch TV or listen to books on tape. He enjoyed me reading cards that had arrived in the mail and just talking. We called the office and he was able to talk with everyone there.

For upcoming visits, the following is some quick advice I received and will pass along, as well. Prior to going, or on the plane ride, write down everything you want to talk to Tommy about so you don't forget something you wanted to ask. I had two pages of yellow legal pad items, and he joked with me going back to the paper, but I really think he enjoyed working through our list.

From a friend of mine that has been through this before, I was told Tommy (as would any patient in his condition) will be looking at my facial expressions to see reactions. Make sure to keep a smile on your face. This is not hard to do; just being around Tommy will keep a smile on your face.

Finally, I was told not to be afraid to touch him or place a hand on his arms, his chest, or even his head. I realize this sounds somewhat unique, but patients in his condition love the touch.

Tommy has a strong positive attitude that he will recover and walk again. He is focused only on positive thoughts and asks the same of everyone. We talked about faith and courage. He definitely has both. We talked about "courage" being the ability to move forward even with a little fear in your heart. He loved that saying and asked me to write it down and hang it up on the wall. I couldn't find any tape, so I will ask the next visitor to take this task on if you see the paper.

He said he was amazed at the number of people concerned about him. He said he didn't realize how many lives he has touched over the years. He also is motivated by his strong faith in God and is encouraged to hear how the blog has turned others into more loyal, faithful followers of Christ.

Tommy is truly an inspiration. The day I was leaving Denver was the ten-year anniversary of the Columbine High School shootings. On the way to the airport, I heard on the radio a statement from the principal of Columbine High School that summed up my visit with Tommy and his state of mind: "It is not the events that happen in our lives that define who we are; it is how we respond to those events."

Sorry this is a little long-winded, but we covered a lot of ground. Feel free to forward on all or parts of this e-mail to those you feel want to hear.

Thanks,

Brian Shaw

Tommy's visitors the next weekend, Mark and Dianne LaRoe, took the time to create a similar update for the next friend. In it, Mark included his prayer requests:

The Lord works in mysterious ways. I changed my seat on the plane this morning at the last minute and sat next to an ordained minister who is a chaplain for one of the NASCAR teams out of Salt Lake City (forgot the family name). He knows all about Craig; they've had drivers there, and he added Tommy to his prayer list. This is the stuff I asked him to pray for:

Sore to heal so they can sit him up.

Increased ventilator weaning.

Continued positive attitude.

Ability to walk out of there in August.

TOUCHING OTHERS

The impact of Tommy's story on others continued to amaze me. For instance, Robyn's neighbor came by to tell her she had been thinking about her. During their conversation, the neighbor said her husband had been reading the blog, which in turn had made him "open his Bible for the first time in many years."

Also, an old friend of Robyn's from Mississippi, Piper Burch, wrote in an e-mail about what the blog had meant to her.

From: Piper Burch

Sent: Sun, 26 Apr 2009 5:30 PM

To: Robyn Sims Van Zandt

Subject: Hello!

Robyn—

I just caught up from the blog and I continue to be uplifted by what is written there! Please tell your husband that he is witnessing to me and teaching me so much from his bed in Denver! I hope you are doing well and able to get rest. I wonder if you ever get back to your home. I can only imagine that you don't want to leave Tommy but that you also want to tend to your boys!

Again—know that you ALL stay in our prayers!

Love,

Piper

We also received a donation to the trust with a note that

said something like this: "I do not know Tommy, but I had heard so much about him from Pat Carrigan and Marty Faulkner in Dallas that I wanted to help." These and the continuing donations with similar notes were inspirational to all of us.

Another example of this profound impact can be seen in the thoughtful note to Robyn from Paul Geater at Transwestern Property Company, where Tommy worked in Dallas.

> **From:** Paul Geater
> **Sent:** Sun, 26 Apr 2009 10:01 AM
> **To:** rsvandandt
> **Subject:** Tommy
>
> Robyn … You do not know me, but I have been following the ongoing saga of Tommy's recovery from the accident. Mr. Jack Elmer of Transwestern sent out an e-mail to Transwestern employees in Dallas back on 2/9/2009. I have been compelled to follow ever since.
>
> I have always thought of myself as being a faithful man, but your family is a true example of what faith is all about. We tend to live our lives in our own little world and tend to be bothered by the really insignificant things in life. As Charles Swindoll once said, life is 10 percent of what happens to you and 90 percent of how you react to it.
>
> Following your story has made me realize what life is truly about: good friends, family, and the quality of your spiritual life. It appears you have all of this and for this you are richly blessed and will continue to be blessed. This is a great testimony of faith and should be shared with all mankind.
>
> Hopefully, you are keeping a daily journal of these

difficult times. Many people will find this inspiring, and I believe God will want you to share this with everyone. You never know … a made-for-TV movie or a traveling ministry to share with others? What a positive inspiration for your boys. There is no better way to raise a child than to share the Word of God and to live the Word every day. Your boys will surely grow up to be mighty men of God. The blessings will reach several generations because of your family's faithfulness and attitude during these trying times.

Keep the faith and I will continue to follow your story as it unfolds. God bless you.

Paul S. Geater

Of course, some days were much tougher than others. Robyn told me about a conversation she had with Tommy on one of those days. Tommy had experienced a very vivid dream the night before in which he and Robyn were loading the car to go on a vacation with the Montgomerys, dear friends from Dallas. Tommy said they both were excited to go, and they were laughing and shouting that God had worked a great miracle because Tommy was walking around and helping to load the car. Then he woke up, still in his bed in Denver.

Robyn sobbed as she told me the story. She told me Tommy was the best man she'd ever met, and God was so good that she couldn't imagine Him letting Tommy stay in the condition he was in at the time.

She apologized for being so upset, and then told me she didn't get upset like this in front of Tommy because she needed to be strong for him. I promised I was always there for her and that she could always talk to me, and I assured her she was doing a great job. In fact, she was doing an incredible job. She was doing a job with strength given to her by the Holy Spirit. And so was Tommy.

My Journal, May 7, 2009

About ten days ago, we had an excited call from one of Tommy's visitors to tell us Tommy had experienced a hiccup. Of course, if this meant anything in his system was "coming back," we were excited. After exploring it with the nurse, however, we weren't sure if it meant progress.

I thought that it was amazing that we were at a point where a single hiccup was a big deal to us. During that same time frame, the respiratory therapist thought that perhaps Tommy was "breathing over" his ventilator at times, perhaps signaling a trend that, over time, would allow him to be weaned off the ventilator.

REFLECTIONS: SEVEN YEARS LATER

By Tommy Van Zandt

When I first started having visitors in Colorado, I was concerned about being able to look as normal as possible. Having a tube coming out of my throat and machines making noise all around me ... it couldn't look too normal.

Within the first thirty seconds together, however, those thoughts went away. They always said they didn't know what to expect. They didn't know if I could talk at all. But I was able to communicate. And they almost always said that within thirty seconds they knew I was "still Tommy." So, once they were able to get their fears out of the way, it allowed me to get any of my concerns out of the way, also.

It was such a blessing to have people around me who were positive and motivating. Quitting was never an option. God never let that creep into my mind.

The Lord had His hands on me from the moment I hit the ground and has been with me throughout this entire journey. He never allowed me to think about giving up. Robyn, the boys, and our entire community rallied around our family. The Lord allowed me to be positive from the beginning. I did not want to go the other direction toward depression, and my close and extended family kept me very positive. With God on your side, giving up is not an option. What a blessing!

Chapter 6

Better Times

Rejoice in the Lord always. I will say it again: Rejoice! Let your
gentleness be evident to all. The Lord is near. Do not be anxious
about anything, but in every situation, by prayer and petition,
with thanksgiving, present your requests to God. And the peace of
God, which transcends all understanding, will guard your hearts
and your minds in Christ Jesus.
PHILIPPIANS 4:4–7 (NIV)

As Tommy settled in at Craig and began to have scheduled
visits from friends, we were able to take some trips that
weren't related to his care.

On the first weekend in May, as Tommy's old friend Scott
Carter visited him in Denver, Vicki and Robyn took Ross (a
junior in high school) on college tours at the University of
Missouri and the University of Kansas.

Jack and I, meanwhile, headed to Circle S, our duck
hunting club near De Witt in the Delta region of Arkansas.
It gave me some great quality time with Jack in a fun and
relaxing environment.

When I picked him up at school that Friday afternoon, he immediately expressed that he was "starving." A quick stop at Mr. Burger on the way out of town was the ticket. He rapidly downed a cheeseburger, fries, and a Dr Pepper. Our drive was more than four hours, so I was ready to eat around 6:30 p.m. We stopped at a Subway, where Jack ate a six-inch sub and potato chips. When we reached the hunting club at 9:00 p.m., he ate three-fourths of a grilled chicken and a big bowl of ice cream with strawberries.

That's three full meals in about five hours. At fourteen and growing daily, Jack seemed like he had a hollow leg!

I have some great photos of both of us enjoying the trip, but I think the best "picture" of our time together is found in an entry in my hunting journal that I asked Jack to write.

Fishing in the Delta, 5/2/09, Jack Van Zandt (age fourteen)
Yesterday it was May 2, our first full day here at Circle S. I woke up not too early, but my regular time, which felt good. Mark and I ate a bowl of cereal and headed off to Benny Petrus' house to go and fish. Uncle Eddie (Drilling) was also there to fish with Benny.

We headed to the reservoir, got into our boats, and started to fish. It was perfect fishing weather, so that is why we caught around twenty-five fish. Both bass and bream. Unfortunately, the bugs got to Uncle Ed's face and he looked like Evander Holyfield after a fight. We gathered up all of our fish, headed back down to the house, and cooked the fish. Our lunch was great.

Mom, Ross, and Vicki were out looking at colleges, so Ross couldn't be here. Also, Dad is still at the hospital in Denver getting fixed up after his accident during the ice storm. We know he is going to get back everything that he once had. Mark and I are about to head out to his farm to see if we can hunt for any varmints. Wish us good luck!

Tommy called during the trip to see how it was going. He told us he was feeling lots of tingling in his body, like electrical impulses. He said he felt like something good was happening inside his body—like it was trying to "reconnect." The feelings were very encouraging, he said, especially because they came on the heels of a couple of bad days when he finally realized the enormity of the healing that needed to occur for him. This was the first time Tommy admitted having "down days" to me.

EARLY MOTHER'S DAY

The week before Mother's Day, we were back in Fayetteville and Robyn was in Denver, when the boys gave Vicki a nice surprise.

Robyn was returning on Friday, and normally we would stay until she was back. But this week we needed to leave a day early. Vicki is on the board of three charter schools that focus on economics, science, technology, engineering, and mathematics, and she has spent years advocating for higher-quality public education for all children. The "eStem" schools honored her by creating the Vicki Saviers Educator of the Year Award, and we needed to return to Little Rock so she could present the inaugural award to a teacher that Thursday.

As we were packing our things, Ross and Jack came into the guest room grinning from ear to ear. They gave Vicki a Mother's Day present, delivered along with very sweet comments of thanks to her for serving as their "second mother."

She cried, and I have to admit that I teared up a little,

too. She told the boys that she knew she had gone from the "cool aunt" to the "tough mom."

I was very proud of the boys. The previous night we had been to dinner with Beth and Marshall (a weekly occurrence), so I figured Beth had helped the boys pick out the gift. It was another reason why Vicki and I so appreciate the fact that our sons, Beth, and Melissa were so thoughtful and helpful to the family over those weeks and months.

My Journal, May 7, 2009

Last night (May 6) Tommy called with very encouraging news. First, he told us that as he was working with the respiratory therapist, Brigitte Trace, trying to breathe via his diaphragm, he actually had some *feeling* in the diaphragm. This was huge. He had felt nothing there since the accident.

He pressed the therapist for what it meant in terms of how long it might take to be weaned off the ventilator. She hedged and said she hated to answer because every patient was different. But when he pressed her further, she said maybe in a month he could be off of it. Or it could be three months. Either way, she felt he could be weaned off of it, which was big news.

Almost immediately, I went into a quiet place to thank God. We had all been praying for this healing many times a day, for more than three months. More specifically, I had been asking the Lord to "turn the switch back on" in Tommy's spine. And it appeared to us at that moment He had done it. Praise the Lord!

The other good news was that the skin

laceration was now nearly healed. The plan is to sit Tommy up in a wheelchair on Monday (May 11). He has been lying on his side, being turned every two and a half hours, for three months. This, too, was a cause for praise.

Today, Robyn called from Denver with more good news. She said Tommy was "eating like a horse." He has been eating solid food for only five or six days, so we are all encouraged by his progress.

SITTING UP

Tommy called the day after Mother's Day to excitedly report that the staff had put him upright in a wheelchair. God's healing of the skin laceration enough for Tommy to sit was an incredible answer to our prayers.

They would put him upright for fifteen minutes, lay him horizontal for three minutes, and then sit him back up for fifteen minutes. The process allowed for the major reorientation of many body functions, including his blood pressure. Tommy said he was upright a total of two hours that first day. He was exhausted but exhilarated.

It was also the first time Tommy had been dressed and in shoes. He said he was continuing to do well eating solid food, although he still needed the feeding tube because he could only get about half the calories he needed by mouth. Finally, he said, he was having lots of spasms in his legs, which he felt was a sign that "something good was happening" to the nerves in his spine.

That same weekend brought more wonderful news for our family: John Mark, our youngest son, became engaged to Melissa Nutt.

Our family loves Melissa. She is a fine woman with a

good sense of humor who fits right in with us. We also love her family. Her father, David Nutt, was one of my prized pledges for Phi Delta Theta when I was one of the rush chairmen at the University of Arkansas. Melissa's mother, Lisa, was Vicki's sorority sister at Chi Omega and Tommy's "big sister" in the fraternity. They are terrific people. We marveled at the small-world coincidence of their engagement, and naturally, we were thrilled at the news.

My Journal, May 20, 2009

Today, we had our second "team" conference call. Tommy's medical team was in his room, along with Robyn. Robyn's brother and I listened in by conference call.

The first part of the meeting focused on Tommy's continuing progress. The antibiotics will be discontinued in two more days. Tommy is eating regular food now, even though the feeding tube is still in place "just in case we need it." The cast is off his right arm and the break there has healed well. The jaw pain is gone. He is getting ready to start on the "FES bike," which provides electrical stimulation to his legs. And the laceration on his rear end is almost fully healed, so sitting in the wheelchair is not affecting it negatively.

It's only been ten days since Tommy was first able to sit upright, and already he is sitting in his chair for up to five hours at a time. He is learning to drive his wheelchair with a "puff straw." He is supposed to blow into the straw a certain way to manipulate the direction and speed of his wheelchair.

Everyone from Denver on the call, however, laughed about his poor driving. His great friend Marty Faulkner had just visited Tommy. Marty reported that Tommy nearly castrated him because of his inability to stop or slow down. Earlier in the week, I had sent him a note teasing him about his poor driving and reminding him that "a man needs to know the length of his vehicle." That's what I had told him as a teenager when he was learning to drive a car, so he knew exactly what I meant.

The last half of the hour-long call was tough. The expected date for Tommy to come home is August 13, and this part of the call dealt with the detailed training program Robyn needs to go through to prepare for taking care of Tommy at home. This included helping Tommy with his "bowel program." The Denver staff highlighted the equipment we would need (electric bed, wheelchair, power lift, special van, etc.).

Dr. Johansen said Tommy had no measured capacity to breathe. They have ordered a study to check his frenetic nerve to see if it is intact to his diaphragm. Tomorrow they start a program called Tetra, which deals with skills needed "in real life." They mentioned the need for home health care and the fact that the insurance will cover very little of it, if any. It will take two people to get Tommy out of bed.

All of this hit me like a slap in the face. It was overwhelming. Tears rolled down my face as I drove around Fayetteville listening on my cell, facing the grim reality of the future.

As much as anyone, and maybe more, I had

been focused on any little progress every day, while not giving up hope. While Tommy's medical team handled the discussion in the most sensitive way possible, it was very hard to hear. Their statement was that we must "plan for the moment and hope for a better tomorrow."

After the call, I phoned Robyn to check on her. Knowing how it had affected me, I couldn't imagine how overwhelming it had been for her. She cried. She expressed anxiety over how much she had to learn and whether she could remember it all.

She said her worst fear is that Tommy has to come home on the ventilator and that it would malfunction with nobody around to help him in that emergency. He could suffocate very quickly. Only yesterday, she said, his ventilator malfunctioned in the hospital, and "half the hospital" came running to help.

I reminded her of all of Tommy's progress since the last call. I told her I felt sure he could come off the ventilator before he came home. And I promised her that Vicki and I would do whatever it took to be in Fayetteville so that she could be in Denver for training.

Meanwhile, Tommy continues to amaze me. He participated in the team call, asking questions and listening closely. Yet he did not seem despondent over issues he would face when he could finally come home.

Toward the end of the meeting, he said, "I want to spend as much time as I can in physical therapy." And then he thanked everyone in the room for the level of care he was receiving. He said he was so impressed, not only with the people, but also the culture of caring at Craig Hospital.

His team said that they were now among the many people who loved Tommy. Several people commented on the terrific support Tommy had received from Robyn and from all of his family and friends.

Later that same evening, Tommy called me without Robyn in the room. He wanted to know if I was OK.

"That was a tough call we had today," he said, "but everything needed to be said."

It was incredible that Tommy could hear all of that difficult news and then call me to make sure I was OK.

"If you and Robyn are OK," he said, "then I am OK."

Robyn's Journal, May 24, 2009, Memorial Day Weekend

Mark and Vicki graciously invited me and the boys to join them at the Little Red River Cabin. It is the perfect haven after a tough week in Denver. It was tough because we had our sobering team meeting. We all have so much hope, but they have to look at where we are, test his diaphragm for the possibility of stimulating it to breathe on his own, and the feasibility of using a FES bike, which provides cardio for Tommy and maybe helps with nerve and muscle stimulation. They do not have many tricks up their sleeve for recovery—just waiting to see what the body recovers. ... God has miraculous healing powers. ... All glory will be to God because it will be

His miraculous hands that heal Tommy, not science or doctors.

It was also hard because the nurses and techs are now trying to train me on the million ways to take care of Tommy. It seems so overwhelming. It is. I have absolutely no interest in medicine or technology. My fear and anxiety first and foremost are for Tommy's safety. He had an emergency when a "plug" got stuck and the tech could not suction it out and they had to "code" Tommy. It seemed as if half the hospital showed up in his room to assist. The tech had to "bag" Tommy, then they used the encephalator and muca mist to thin his secretions. All very scary. And how do I do this alone at home??? Also, they just started getting Tommy up in his chair. His blood pressure dropped very low and he passed out several times, but now they just immediately lean him back in his chair to bring his BP back up.

We took him to Chili's for a field trip—so much preparation, attention. ... He got food stuck in his throat. ... How do you do the Heimlich with someone who has a trach???? Good to do these things, but no fun really for anybody!!! This is so hard. But Tommy is at peace and so sweet. God will provide us with the strength to get through this stronger and better. He will never leave me or forsake me or Tommy.

On a positive note, travel has gotten easier, I have gotten my routine down, people continue to reach out to help us. Tommy is affecting people's lives in such a positive way—friends and staff! Mark and Vicki are so helpful and supportive. The Dallas fundraiser is shaping up to be a big deal. We are

figuring out our summer calendars. Tommy's skin is
doing very well. We are waiting on the Lord. He is
good, faithful, and holy. Jack is maturing and Ross
is willing to be helpful to us! Praise be to God! I love
you!

MOMENTS FOR MELTDOWNS

All of us had to stay strong in front of Tommy and Robyn,
but periodically, each of us had a meltdown.

One week, Vicki was exhausted and frustrated. Living
most of the time in Fayetteville had caused her to disengage
from her routine. She couldn't attend her normal activities
for the board of the eStem charter schools. And she had
to decline an invitation to hand out graduation certificates
at Pulaski Technical College, where she also serves on the
board. She yearned to get back to these and other volunteer
activities that were her work. At one point, she told me, "My
life sucks right now."

I had felt that type of frustration about a month earlier,
when I experienced my own form of a meltdown. When it
was Vicki's turn, I did my best to encourage her to work a
few interesting and fun things into her schedule. I could
cover the duties with Ross and Jack, I assured her.

It didn't do much good. She felt compelled to drive
carpool, prepare sack lunches, wash clothes and sheets,
or drive Robyn to and from the airport that was forty-five
minutes away. This was her job now, she said.

On top of helping with Tommy's family, she was working
hard to assist with John Mark and Melissa's wedding plans.
They were getting married in New Orleans. We had lived
there years ago, so we had friends and connections who could
help. But it was a lot for Vicki to handle right then, and I was

proud of the way she persevered through the frustrations.

Everyone dealt with Tommy's situation differently. Mud constantly felt "in the dark" with what was going on with him. Part of this was that he was so far away in Denver, while she was home in Little Rock.

The uncertainty of Tommy's future was particularly hard on her. She did not check e-mail or the blog (she once said she couldn't because she "wasn't a member" of the Internet). She got frustrated because she thought Vicki wasn't telling her everything that was happening—both with Tommy and with all of our family. This was all understandable. Tommy is her only son, and she was grieving.

Vicki was sometimes overwhelmed, not only because she had lost control of her normal life, but also because everyone leaned on her for support. She is very strong and decisive, so naturally, we all depend on her. However, some days she reached her emotional maximum.

Mud depended on and called her several times each day. Ross and Jack looked to her for everything from buying khaki pants to filling out the enrollment forms for camp. I'm sure I leaned on her too hard sometimes—less for emotional support, but more often just to try to spend time together alone.

Robyn naturally needed someone to talk to. She always had to be so strong in front of Tommy, so she needed an outlet in Vicki.

My Journal, May 22, 2009

We all have our down periods, but I'm well aware that, given our situation, each of us is doing great. Tommy keeps a positive and encouraging attitude, which is really a miracle when you think about all

that he's facing. And that attitude not only keeps
him going, but it lifts the rest of us, as well.

I believe the human inclination when something
so seemingly unfair happens to us is to get mad—at
God, at people, at everything. Many people respond
with bitterness and depression. Clearly, God's hand
is helping each of us avoid this each day, one day at
a time.

God's hand is on my new friend, Dean, too,
but I see a stark contrast whenever I think of how
a similar situation is playing out in Dean's family.
Around Christmas, just a couple of months before
Tommy's accident, Dean's thirty-two-year-old son
Kevin lost the use of his entire upper body, including
the ability to breathe on his own. Kevin was in the
Army, serving in Iraq, and about to come home after
two years on duty there. No one knows what caused
his condition, but obviously it's incredibly hard on
Dean and his family.

Kevin has a young wife who is expecting their
first child. Now, he is in a hospital in Seattle trying to
make sense of everything that's happening to him.
Dean says there are times when he won't speak to
anyone, including his wife. Last week, he was put on
suicide watch.

Kevin's reaction, sadly, is very typical. According
to the RAND Center for Military Health Policy
Research, 20 percent of the veterans who served
in Iraq or Afghanistan suffer from either major
depression or post-traumatic stress disorder. Later,
I read on the Christopher Reeve Foundation web
page that victims of paralysis from any source are
two to three times as likely to become depressed.

Depression is a very real medical problem, and it requires medical treatment.

My good friend, Wayne Moore, was telling me about a book—*God on Mute*—that helped him reconcile with God after he learned that two of his three beautiful sons have type 1 diabetes. When I told Wayne about Dean's son, he immediately ordered two copies of the book. I gave one to Dean and asked him to take the other to Kevin. Maybe this will be one way for God to reveal Himself to that hurting family. Later, on a couple of occasions, I met Kevin in person. I like him. I felt immense sympathy for both Kevin and Dean. Thankfully, Kevin is receiving intense medical treatment in Seattle.

I haven't talked to anyone else in our family about Dean's son. With all of the concerns about everything else going on with Tommy and the family, we did not need to add worries about potential depression.

REFLECTIONS: SEVEN YEARS LATER

By Tommy Van Zandt

When you're in the hospital for such a long stretch, you can't help but spend a lot of time with your own thoughts. It's easy to see how people go really inward and end up battling depression.

Thankfully, I had great support from my family and friends, and my nurses at Craig were invaluable. They were truly angels to my physical and emotional well-being.

One in particular, my main nurse, was Courtney Long. I'm still in touch with her. I've told her this: I think she single-handedly helped me get beyond the point of being so sick that I was unaware of what my condition really was.

And she just treated me like a normal human being. She brought joy to me every day. I gained self-confidence. No matter my condition, she reminded me that I was still human … still me. We laughed together. We cried together. We talked about our faith or, in her case, lack thereof.

She had consciously turned into a nonbeliever. She abandoned her faith. Near the end of my time at Craig, she became open to exploring her faith again. It did not take her long to get back in the fold.

I have lots of funny stories about Courtney. For

instance, when she'd roll me to the shower, she wouldn't just go to the shower. She and her assistant, Dana Martinez (another incredible angel to me), would roll me by the nurses' stations and all around and yell, "Tommy's naked, Tommy's naked." I was totally appalled. It got to be a big joke around the hospital. Dana would read books to me while she fed me dinner each night, sacrificing her own meal time. What a gift!

Chapter 7

Tommy's Clearinghouse

For where two or three gather in my name, there am I with them.
MATTHEW 18:20 (NIV)

Each time one of Tommy's friends visited Denver, everyone looked forward to reading the e-mail report circulated by Paul James. He began calling it "Tommy's Clearinghouse." It not only updated everyone on Tommy's weekly progress, but also helped prepare the next visitor with what to expect.

Going to visit a close friend whose life has been "flipped" can bring on a wave of emotions. *Will I know what to say? Will my body language say something that offends him? Will I be overcome with emotion? Can I be strong and encouraging for my friend?* But these regular e-mails helped people deal with their apprehensions. Of course, once they arrived for a visit, Tommy also put them at ease.

One of the more hilarious accounts came from Marty Faulkner, a friend of Tommy's from college. They also were roommates as bachelors in Dallas, living on Normandy Street in a place they nicknamed "The Beachhead."

(Side note: Link is Tommy's middle name.)

From: Marty Faulkner

Sent: Tuesday, May 19, 2009 8:41 AM

To: Paul James

Subject: Faulkner Factoids from TVZ visit to Denver

Well, this is what I saw with my eyes this past weekend in Denver while visiting our friend Thomas Link Van Zandt. He's obviously a man of strong faith, fortitude, positive, great sense of humor, and the same guy that I've known for thirty-two years. He's challenged, but he's also the guy to face the challenge. By the way, I love him.

Here we go with the happenings:

I got to the hospital around 11:00 a.m. Saturday morning. I reached his doorway and he is already in his new battery-operated wheelchair and he hears my voice and gives the same response that I've heard for many years, "Faulk, get in here." His tech Tina was finishing up the tech things in his chair and gave me instructions with buttons to contact nurses if we needed them.

Well, she walks out and within five minutes I look at Link and his gigantic eyes are popping and I read his lips: "I can't breathe." Nice first ten minutes with my friend after I get out of a cab. I proceeded to start hitting buttons and then the Red Army hit the door flying in response. I mean about five nurses and a doctor in track shoes, and they mean business. We were all good after they fixed the vent tubing/hose that had disconnected from the portable vent on the wheelchair. Neither Link nor I panicked.

On to hallways and a little NASCAR bumping off the walls and rubbing paint, as TVZ and the nurses called it. He's going to be good after more practice in this chair.

It's awesome for him because he's sitting up and seeing people and the world.

We then went to the lunch room where he proceeded to eat a sloppy joe, veggies, salad, and some fruit like a big horse in the pasture. He can put away the groceries again, folks. The solid foods, sitting up, and the wheelchair make a vast difference in my eyes.

From there we talked and covered the globe with conversation for five to six hours and also went back for dinner. I left about 7:30 that night to cab-it back to the hotel. To say the least, a meaningful and eventful day.

Sunday morning, I got to his room at 8:00 a.m. He was just waking up and he said he slept like a log. He ate a little breakfast, and then we just talked some more. And, man, he is with it talking. And I mean with it. He still had to listen to me a little. His surfer next-door neighbor, Eddie from California, dropped in to chat for a good while. Interesting man and worldly.

Then his nurses, Cindy and Tina, got him ready for the transfer from the bed to the chair for our road trip to the lunchroom. When he couldn't stop the wheelchair, he proceeded to ram tables/chairs and me across the room a bit. We all laughed and I asked him if he was trying to wreck my jewelry store. He's still got the same humor, folks. We then went back to the room for more talk before I departed. We shared a very meaningful prayer and I left.

We talked on the phone with Mud, Chuck Roscopf, Pat Carrigan, Fred Whistle, Mark Saviers, Robyn, Dr. Al Gordon, and Pat Burnham during my visit. He enjoyed visiting with all.

I am so impressed with the staff. Dana, Cindy, and

Tina are the ones that I got to know. They are fabulous and of course they all love Mr. Casanova. He's still got it with the lassies. Don't worry, Robyn, he just likes to work the room to see if he still has it.

All in all, I'll sum it up that he is stronger and ready for the challenge ahead. If anyone can tackle this, it is TVZ. Wow is he strong mentally. I can't wait to see him again and to get the laugh machine going.

I am so honored to call him my friend, my guy Thomas Link Van Zandt.

Marty Faulkner

My Journal, May 20, 2009

This week it was my turn to pick up Robyn at the airport in Northwest Arkansas. Robyn had a good flight, and although she was tired, she seemed mellow and fairly relaxed.

She told me Tommy has so many new friends on the medical team that it's difficult in the course of the whole week for he and Robyn to have any time together alone. At one point, she asked for thirty minutes of time for just the two of them, and even then, they were interrupted by someone who did not know about the request.

Robyn described one nurse who knew Tommy was a man of faith, so she told him she had prayed on the way in to work—as if that was an unusual thing for her. Another nurse told Robyn that Tommy was one of the few people ever in her care who actually "gave more to her than she gave to the patient." One of the techs had said that if Tommy would move to Denver, she would care for him at home for free.

The other topic on the return from the airport was the preparation for Tommy to come home. Our "team meeting" on this subject had been weighing heavily on Robyn. She cried about the worries she had, especially if Tommy was still on the ventilator when he came home in mid-August.

I did my best to assure her that I felt strongly that he would not still be on the ventilator when he came home—even though I was always careful to qualify it as my feeling and not something the Lord had told me. And if for some reason he was still on the ventilator, we would deal with it as a team with her and take every precaution to be prepared.

Finally, we discussed the need to modify their house to make it handicap accessible for Tommy. I promised I would help with that. I assured her it was not a big problem and that we would be ready.

THE BOOK OF JOY

One way God helped me deal with our situation was through our beloved neighborhood Bible study that typically meets at our home in Little Rock. I was able to attend several of the meetings in April through June as we read and discussed Philippians, which is often described as the Bible's "book of joy."

It is hard to describe the strength and perspective this study provided—not just for me, but also for many of the other guys. For instance, a money manager in our group was dealing with the daily meltdown in the economy and the financial markets in the recession.

"I don't know about you guys," he said, "but I could use a little joy right about now."

John Ramsey, who had just moved to Little Rock and was new to our group that semester, had lived through the hell of being accused of the murder of his beautiful daughter, JonBenét Ramsey, in Colorado. He and his wife lived with the suspicions for many years, and she died from cancer before the district attorney admitted she and her husband were no longer suspects. Now John works to promote DNA sampling at crime scenes so injustices like his are not thrust upon innocent people. He never mentioned his background as he sat quietly through the study week after week, but my guess is that he "needed a little joy," as well.

One of the key points in Philippians is that we should not derive our joy from our circumstances in this world. Instead, real joys come from our relationship with Jesus Christ and the resulting fact that, as believers, we have already become "citizens of heaven."

This discussion reminded me of a devotional I had heard years earlier by Lorne Sanny, president of The Navigators. As Christians, he said, we live every day with one foot in today and the other foot in eternity.

I felt like our situation with Tommy was living with one foot in today (i.e., having to modify his house) and the other foot in hope. Craig Hospital was preparing us to deal with the hard realities of Tommy's condition to bring him home, yet we continued to pray and to have hope. It was a difficult balance as we approached the fourth full month after the injury.

SHARK FISHING

One evening in late May, Vicki and I had the pleasure of taking Ross, Jack, Marshall, and Beth to dinner at Bordinos, one of our favorite restaurants in Fayetteville. It was a beautiful evening, so we sat outside on the patio to enjoy the late spring weather.

Ross and Jack love to be with Beth and Marshall. The four of them were going to dinner almost weekly, so they knew each other very well. Of course, the boys had known each other as cousins all of their lives, but all the other extra time together since February had made them really close.

During the conversation that evening Beth mentioned she was flying to South Carolina the next weekend to celebrate her sister's thirtieth birthday with her. She said the two of them had hired a fishing guide to take them shark fishing. They had never gone before, but that was her sister's choice for her birthday present.

When she said the guide wanted to take them fishing at night, my first thought was that it wasn't wise for two beautiful young women to go out with a fishing guide they did not know at night. Obviously, Jack had the same thought.

"Don't do it!" he said. "He might try to make a move on you!"

We all had a good laugh and really enjoyed that dinner. The girls went fishing anyway (I am not sure if they went at night), and they caught some small sharks to prove they could do it.

A few days after that dinner, Marshall and Beth took Jack to buy new boots for summer camp at Deer Hill in Colorado in July. Marshall and John Mark had both been to that camp as teenagers, so Vicki and I felt it was important for Jack to have that experience, as well.

Marshall's coaxing to break in the boots and to get

prepared for the hiking meant a lot to Jack. We were thankful for the positive influence Marshall and Beth had on the boys at a very important time in their lives.

GOSSIP GONE WILD

Tommy Foltz, one of our longtime family friends, got an alarming phone call one day from someone in Fort Smith, the town where Tommy and Vicki and I all grew up. The caller had heard that Tommy had died.

Foltz tried without success to call me, then drove by Mud's house and our house to see if there were a lot of cars there.

When I saw several missed calls from him, I knew something was up. And when I returned his call, I emphatically explained that Tommy was fine and, in fact, was feeling much better in recent weeks.

Foltz was furious and promised to "set the record straight" in Fort Smith and stop the gossip. My worry was that someone in Fort Smith would hear the rumor and call Mud to offer their condolences, which of course would have upset her terribly.

Mud had told us on multiple occasions people had approached her in public places and had said inappropriate things that made her feel bad. Vicki and I talked with her about how to respond to certain probing questions to limit the damage of tough conversations, but it was never easy.

Just about the time these kinds of frustrations would wear on us, the Lord would send us encouragement from the many more people who were sensitive and kind. One such timely encouragement came from Tommy's friend Trey Hollis on the first of June.

Robyn and Tommy about two years before the injury.

Mark and Tommy at Crested Butte about six months before the injury.

About 2005 back row: Tommy, Jack, Ross, John Mark, Mark, Marshall, Vicki; front row: Robyn, Big Dad, Mud

Tommy and Jack in the duck blind—about two weeks before the accident.

Jack on our fishing trip to the Arkansas Delta.

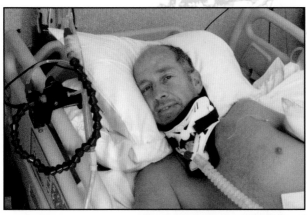

On my first visit to Craig Hospital in Denver, Tommy was still so sick that he could not remember two weeks later that I had come at all.

The skybridge at Craig Hospital in Denver.

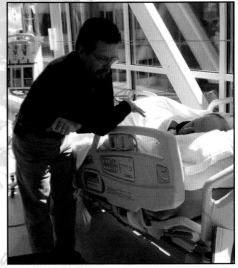

Dr. John James encouraging Tommy on the skybridge.

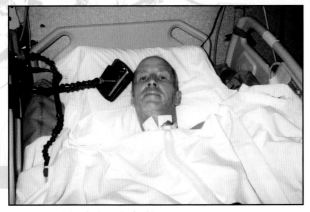

Tommy with his beloved Blackberry.

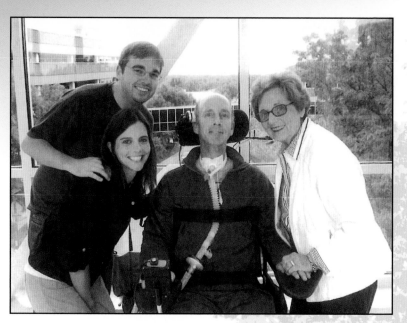

Marshall, Beth, Tommy, and Mud at Craig Hospital.

David Roth, one of several close friends in "Tommy's Clearinghouse," who came to visit in Craig Hospital.

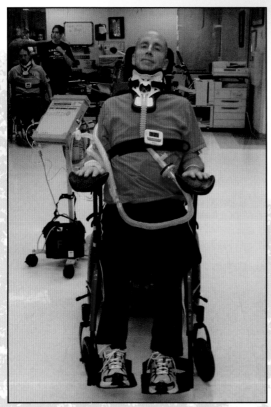

May 11, 2009—Sitting upright for the first time in three months.

Mud with Ross. See why we all love Mud?

Robyn's birthday party in 2017—Mary Collins Saviers (age 5), Russell Saviers (age 3), Mark, Robyn, Tommy and Vicki.

Rick Roblee, Roy Clinton, Tony Sherman, Mary Beth Sherman, Trey Hollis—
Celebrating with Tommy at his first Razorbacks game after the accident.

Marshall, Brian Shaw, T. J. Lefler, Mark, and David Erstine with Tommy at the first "Tommy's Nite Out" in Fayetteville.

Jack, Robyn, Tommy, and Ross in 2015.

The tree where Tommy fell—ugly and barren in wintertime.

The tree in summertime, beautiful and reborn.

"But blessed is the one who trusts in the LORD,
whose confidence is in him.
They will be like a tree planted by the water
that sends out its roots by the stream.
It does not fear when heat comes; its leaves are always green.
It has no worries in a year of drought and never fails to bear fruit."
(Jeremiah 17:7-8, NIV)

From: Hollis, Trey K
Sent: Monday, June 1, 2009 7:50 AM
To: Paul James
Subject: Tommy Visit Report ...

Paul,

Below is my Tommy Visit Report ☺

Let me start by saying that I was blessed beyond imagination to spend two days with such a strong man of faith, character, hope, courage, wit, and joy. I have always known that Tommy is special, but I am amazed at the impact one man can have on so many people. I know I speak for most of us who know Tommy when I say he has become a source of hope and encouragement for everyone he has and will encounter. Clearly God's hand is at work in his life.

Tommy and I spoke at length about his gift of being able to quickly make real and meaningful "connections" with people. Tommy seems inspired to use whatever situation he is in (now and in the future) to connect with people and share a story of unwavering faith in God and love and kindness for everyone he encounters. Hearing Tommy's enthusiasm for "reaching" people is truly inspirational.

The emotions I experienced while spending time with Tommy ran the gamut. Of course, his wit and sense of humor are perhaps his most endearing qualities. When I first arrived at Craig Hospital, there was a representative from a wheelchair manufacturer there doing specs on a chair for Tommy.

While making sure all the measurements were accurate, the representative mentioned that Tommy's head seemed to be leaning a little to the left. Of course, that prompted Tommy to respond immediately with one of his many one-liners. He said, "I am not sure if you heard or not, but I broke my neck, which may have something to do with my head leaning!"

We all laughed hysterically. Tommy's gift of using humor to make people comfortable was at work from the second I walked in!!

There are many more extremely funny stories I took away, and Tommy and I laughed most of the time I was there. Sometimes Tommy laughed so hard that I was concerned the ventilator would not be able to keep up with him!

As you can imagine, Tommy has become the de facto "Mayor of Craig Rehab!" Now that he is mobile, he has begun making his rounds up and down the halls. It should not surprise anyone that Tommy enjoys giving more than receiving. In fact, he could not wait to take one of the many flower arrangements he received to his next-door neighbor to make her day!

I brought Tommy a lot of sweets/cookies/candy, etc. I fully expect he will get more joy out of giving it all away than eating it himself! That's just the kind of guy he is!

On Saturday evening, Tommy decided he wanted to have a little Mexican Fiesta in Room 312 (Tommy's Hacienda!). While his attentive staff was helping him clean up/shower, I ran to a Mexican restaurant and returned with enough food to feed me, Tommy, and most of the on-duty staff (Dana, Maria, and Tina, aka Tommy's Harem!). Let me tell you, Tommy's appetite is as strong as ever! He can put away the groceries! In addition to three hearty meals a day, he was not shy about asking for cookies and malted milk balls between meals!

While there was plenty of laughter and joy, we also

had some pretty deep and serious discussions. One of the things Tommy prays for (and wants others praying for) is discernment and clarity around how God wants to use Tommy's gifts and situation to minister to others. Tommy is content with whatever his situation is or will be but wants to understand how God wants to use him to reach others. Tommy seems passionate about figuring this out!

I know Tommy, and everyone aware of his injury, continues to pray diligently for his ongoing recovery. But take joy in knowing Tommy is aware of all the many miracles that are occurring in the midst of his recovery journey.

I went to Denver this weekend hoping to help Tommy in some small way. Wouldn't you know that my contribution to Tommy was allowing him to give me hope and inspiration (which is pleasing to him)? His joy is in helping others, and I return to Fayetteville with a greater understanding of the kind of man I want to be!

To God be the glory.

Trey K. Hollis

Notes like this provided refreshment on a tough day.

It seemed that the cycle went like this: Tommy would encourage and strengthen good friends like Trey, who in turn would do the same for our family and for Tommy's inner circle of friends. These encouragements would be reflected on the blog, which reached hundreds of others who followed it daily.

The cycle also worked in reverse, where the Lord would strengthen one of us, and we in turn could encourage Tommy or someone else in the family. The love being expressed to us, or from us, made the rounds daily. To me, this was a miracle every day, expressed in hundreds of ways over the months.

Marc Myers, one of my Dallas business partners and also a friend of thirty years, put it this way: "It's like hundreds of protons bouncing into each other, colliding and providing positive energy. Some of them bounce out and make an impact somewhere else that you don't ever even know about, causing positive implications elsewhere."

TURNING THE ENCOURAGEMENT TABLES

On Saturday, June 6, it was my turn to encourage Tommy. I was sitting alone on our patio at home on a beautiful morning when he called and asked what I was doing.

"I'm sitting here being thankful and thinking about you," I said.

It was true.

At my request, he gave me a quick medical report. He said he'd been experiencing some strange side effects as the nurses allowed him more time each day to sit upright in his wheelchair. He became very cold in the afternoons, he said, and one day his body temperature had dropped to 92 degrees. Several times his blood pressure had dropped precipitously, down to one-half to one-third of normal rates. He started getting headaches again in the afternoon, but these wouldn't go away with Tylenol (Tommy wouldn't take narcotics).

None of this made him feel really bad, he said, but it "was just weird." Dr. Johansen didn't seem worried; he said they were neurological side effects from his condition.

After hearing that, I was excited to tell Tommy about my walk the previous Friday morning with Rick Massey, a neighbor with whom I crossed paths on my regular exercise route.

Rick is a successful lawyer-turned investment banker-turned business executive. After helping engineer the sale of Alltel to Verizon, and while awaiting the closing, Rick had been stricken with what I heard was a stroke in his spine. This put him in the hospital for a month and resulted in paralysis from the waist down for a few months. Yet, here I was walking with him only six months later.

I told Tommy how I had observed Rick over the months, first on a walker, then on a cane, now on a steady, slightly halting gait on our walk together.

Rick has always been a workout fanatic. He told me about his weekly routine, including a three-hour "pool crawl" on some days. I told him all about Tommy, including his positive mental attitude and strong faith. When I asked Rick what advice he would give Tommy, his response was, "He's doing it. Keep at it. That's what it will take."

The story encouraged Tommy and prompted him to tell me about Ross's experience just the week before at Boys State. Ross had been buoyed by an inspirational talk from one of the speakers—a quadriplegic who told his story.

Ross approached him afterward and told him about his dad, asking what advice he would share with Tommy if he were talking with him. The man looked squarely at Ross and said, "Believe."

As we began to wrap up this long conversation, Tommy told me he was glad we had talked because he felt better and needed some positive encouragement. He said that he had been "a little discouraged" the last few days because his progress had been so slow lately.

I couldn't believe I was hearing Tommy finally admit he felt "a little discouraged." It made me feel good that he could share that with me. He was so strong to everyone, day after day, week after week. He had to let down with someone. I begged him to call me anytime, night or day, about anything on his mind. We both felt better after that call.

The next Tuesday, we got some great news. The long-ordered test of Tommy's phrenic nerves, one on each side leading to the diaphragm, was positive. Each nerve was intact! Only after the test did we learn that the physicians thought, due to the extent of his injury, this positive result was unlikely.

Tommy had called Vicki and me with the good news the day of the test. On that call, he told me he sensed that the "techs here had given up on me" with the breathing exercises. This was huge for us. It meant that now it was possible to implant the pacemaker-like device that would stimulate the phrenic nerves, which over time could stimulate breathing, allowing the possibility of being off the ventilator for a period of time.

I had asked Tommy a dozen questions, knowing he had asked his caregivers all of the same ones. "When can we get the pacemaker?" "Does it always work?" "How long can you be off the ventilator, if it works?"

As always, the answers were vague and filled with uncertainties. However, we were learning to be thankful, one day at a time, in the ultimate walk of faith. As Tommy put it, "I was needing some good news, and the Lord gave it to us today."

Vicki and I rejoiced and thanked the Lord for this encouragement. Ever since the test had been ordered, many people knew about it via the blog and had been praying for this result. As my sister, Ann, observed at the time, it was amazing that the things we had prayed for together (aided by the blog requests), like healing for the skin laceration and now the phrenic nerves, had been answered.

Common prayer is powerful indeed. We had daily proof of this fact.

REFLECTIONS: SEVEN YEARS LATER

By Tommy Van Zandt

The visits from friends while I was at Craig were all super special. Many people traveled long distances and at great expense to see me. It was humbling.

Tony Sherman visited several times, and one of those really stands out in my memory. It was in early spring and the trees were starting to bud. It was getting up to 75 or 80 degrees outside in Denver. The thing I wanted most was to get out of the hospital and get outside in the warmth of the sun.

My injury caused the temperature gauges in my body to go haywire. I'm a few degrees cooler than most people, so I'm chilly all of the time. For the first three months, I was not able to get in a wheelchair because of my pressure wounds. I had to be in bed all the time, and I was in a cold hospital.

My nurse, Courtney Long, convinced the doctor I needed a prescription for some Vitamin D. She and Tony rolled me in my hospital bed down the hall, down the elevator, through the cafeteria, out to the courtyard, and into the sun. Tony had ordered pizza. We ate pizza outside in the sun.

I will never forget that. It was one of the high points of my stay in Colorado. And it's still a high point for me to sit in the sun.

It meant the world to me to be able to see people who were close friends, and even those I might not have seen for a few years. Just to get outside of myself and outside of my own thoughts, my own hospital room, my own rehabilitation.

We talked about our friendships. We talked about faith. It was wonderful to be able to pray with those who came and brought prayers to me.

Almost everyone who came would order food for me—whatever I wanted. And we would sit and eat and visit and laugh. Mainly laughing. It was a gift.

I remember several guys coming in and crying. Tears would flow when they looked at me. I took it as tears of joy, not sadness. It gave me a lot of strength and the will to persevere and be healthy so that nobody would have to worry about me or feel sorry for me or have pity on me.

Chapter 8

Helping Hands

For I know the plans I have for you ... plans to prosper you and
not to harm you, plans to give you hope and a future.
JEREMIAH 29:11 (NIV)

Vicki and I headed to Dallas on June 11, 2009, for Tommy's Nite Out—the first major fundraiser for the Van Zandt Family Trust.

Tommy's former coworkers at Transwestern Property Company organized and sponsored the event. It had been ten years since Tommy had worked at Transwestern, but he still had close ties to several people there.

Kim Butler, Riis Christensen, Jack Eimer, and Randy Garrett led a team of about thirty employees who worked for weeks on the party.

The concept was to challenge companies in the commercial real estate industry in a fun competition to raise money for Tommy's family. It culminated in a big celebration at Victory Plaza (where the Dallas Mavericks play) featuring three bands and a silent auction.

The *Dallas Business Journal* and *The Dallas Morning News* both wrote articles in advance of the event, and the team at Transwestern also used letters, e-mails, and the blog to get the word out. Even though it had to be moved inside because of the weather, it was a huge success and provided a blueprint for a similar fundraiser that's still held most years in Arkansas.

Vicki and I could feel the energy in the air as we walked across Victory Plaza to the W Hotel for a reception before the party. The Tommy's Nite Out logo flashed across gigantic billboard screens, and I began to feel nervous as we approached the hotel.

Jack Eimer had called the day before to ask me to say a few words at the reception, which was for organizers and contributors. I am not normally intimidated by speaking to a group; however, these people had done such a special thing for our family that I wanted my words to be just right without my getting too emotional.

After thanking Transwestern corporately, then Kim, Riis, Jack, and Randy individually, I also thanked all of the people there who were contributing to the trust. I told them their gifts were "manna from heaven" for the family. God was providing for the family out of love and had used all of the donors as a vehicle to supply the gifts. My brief conclusion provided an update on Tommy and his family. I quoted Tommy as saying, "I have the faith and the fight to get better."

The party itself began at 7:00 p.m. and was immediately jammed with more than nine hundred people spread across two big rooms upstairs and down. The bands played continuously, one after the other, in the downstairs room. It was fantastic. We could not believe the level of planning and preparation that had occurred to generate this monumental success.

My old friend (and fraternity big brother) Carl Cross, a transplanted Arkansan in Dallas, and his wife, Elizabeth, can attest to the fun. They danced long and hard. When he called me the next day with a gravelly, post-party voice, he told me he hoped he didn't embarrass me and that his knees were sore. Elizabeth had asked him that next morning, "Do you have any idea how a fifty-six-year-old man looks when doing the splits?"

Carl was one of the special friends who had religiously called to check on Tommy over the months. To him and many others, the party provided an emotional release after months of intensity and prayers for the family.

The Transwestern team told me planning and executing the event brought them much closer to each other. In particular, one team member used the work as a positive distraction that helped him deal with a difficult divorce.

It was clear to me that the huge commitment to help Tommy and Robyn's family had also been a blessing to the planners themselves. It was an example of Christ's teaching that one is more blessed to give than to receive.

A few moments in particular stood out from that first Tommy's Nite Out.

One was when Ross thanked everyone for helping his family. At seventeen, he was unusually mature and articulate.

Another very emotional moment was a two-minute video of Tommy and Robyn. Tommy said he was doing fine and even cracked a few jokes. The video had been created the previous week by Pat Carrigan and his good friend Kurt Neale, who spent nearly two days in Denver filming. It not only was a huge hit at the party, but also an invaluable keepsake for the family.

A third highlight was the talk delivered by Bret Bunnett, the honorary chair of Tommy's Nite Out. Bret is a very successful entrepreneur who runs Capstar, a real estate company in Dallas. He also is paralyzed, injured eighteen years earlier in a diving accident. He spoke about the financial needs of a person with a spine injury—a $45,000 van, a $30,000 wheelchair, etc.—all adding up, in his estimation, to $500,000 to $1 million in the first year alone.

In the days following Tommy's Nite Out, we all felt inspired by the love and the generosity of so many people. The party raised more than $175,000 for the family trust. More than the money, the outpouring of support caused several of us to reflect on how good people can be.

Ross told me he couldn't really describe how he felt, because he had never had such a feeling before. He said he couldn't believe so many people would help his dad, even though they had moved away from Dallas more than ten years ago. The whole event left an everlasting impression.

It was about this time that our dear friends Rainer and Marsha Twiford gave us another huge boost.

Rainer and I met through our wives in New Orleans some thirty years ago. He is such a talent that I almost immediately tried to hire him away from Jones–Walker Law Firm, and eventually he came to work with me at the Trammell Crow Company. The four of us have been fast friends ever since. We are godparents to their youngest son, Will.

Rainer and Marsha had never met Tommy or Robyn, but still they offered to help put Ross and Jack through school. We set up 529 accounts for each of the boys. For the next few years, the Twifords quietly contributed to these college funds (and, in Jack's case, high school, too). Vicki and I contributed, too, but we were led by Rainer and Marsha in this effort. We will never forget their quiet, far-sighted generosity.

RENOVATIONS

During the second week in June, the team of Cody Crawford (contractor), Mark Sugg (architect/home builder), and Jill Hollis (decorator) assembled to design the alterations needed to make the Van Zandt home accessible for Tommy. These were all good family friends who had volunteered to help.

Tommy was scheduled to leave Craig Hospital on August 13, so it was time to go to work. Doors needed to be widened, ramps built, a closet converted into a shower, bathroom alterations made, and a generator installed to provide backup power for the ventilator.

After Mark met with Robyn to hear her thoughts and to get the specifications sent by Craig, he designed the general scope of work and went over it with the team at the Van Zandt house.

I called Cody the next week to get his impressions. He said the job wasn't too complicated, so it should only take two or three weeks. When I asked him to send me an estimated cost, he said there would be no cost to the family. He had assembled a team of good-hearted subcontractors, he said, and all of them would donate their time, the materials, or both. His company, Crawford Construction, would cover any other cost.

I immediately objected. Cody and his wife already had sent a very generous donation to the family trust. Plus, I knew the generator alone could cost $6,000 to $8,000. My best guess was that Cody would be giving another $15,000 to $20,000 to the family with this gesture. It was simply too much for him to do with a fairly new company and a young baby of his own.

We agreed to table that discussion, but I hung up with another overwhelming feeling of the goodness of people.

It made me personally want to be more generous. And it made me thank God for His people.

My Journal, June 20, 2009

Marshall and Beth flew with Mud to Denver from Tulsa over the weekend to visit Tommy there for the first time. It was a huge help for her to travel with them.

She's always been an anxious traveler, but on this occasion she was unusually so. She worried about the drive to Fayetteville in the heat of summer. She worried about whether the door would be locked at Tommy's house when she arrived. She didn't know what to pack.

When Vicki told me all of this, it was clear the real issue was her overall nervousness in seeing Tommy in the hospital. This was understandable, for sure. When I asked Tommy how their visit was going, he speculated she was nervous because the whole scene in the hospital reminded her too much of all of those years in and out of the hospital with Big Dad.

Anyway, she did fine on her trip. Vicki and I talked about how good Beth and Marshall had been to all of us, including Mud, in taking her with them. Beth has a sweet, fun spirit about her, and Mud loves being with her.

Both Beth and Marshall couldn't wait to call Vicki and me to tell us funny Mud stories. On this trip, Mud got forty-five minutes from home before she remembered that she forgot to put her suitcase in the car. They turned around to retrieve it. Not long after they arrived (late) at the airport in Tulsa, Mud was paged on the intercom system because she had left her billfold in the candy shop.

DUMPING THE CREDIT CARD DEBT

The medical bills had been rolling in for months, and each time they came, they were forwarded right away to Blue Cross/Blue Shield.

By the end of June, we had seen a bill for the surgery: $36,800. Just the ICU "room and board" at Washington Regional cost $327,060.85, and that was only for the first thirty days. I could not imagine what six months at Craig Hospital would cost. Tommy's policy had a $5 million lifetime cap, which at this spending rate we would probably need.

Each month I braced for a major argument with the insurance company over what services were provided, why they were provided, or some other reason for them not paying. The arguments never came. Blue Cross/Blue Shield handled each one promptly and billed us only for the $6,000 deductible. We were really grateful to them, to say the least.

The last week in June, after receiving some help from Brian Rosenthal at the Rose Law Firm on how to reduce some of Tommy and Robyn's credit card payments, Vicki and I paid those bills, as well as their property taxes. Brian would not let us pay him for helping us.

We didn't feel it was appropriate for the trust to pay these bills. The donors were giving to help the family with bills coming out of the hardship of the accident, not to pay old debts.

We saw this as another opportunity to help financially as

family members, and we were thankful we could do it. God had blessed us in 2008 with two very profitable real estate deals that easily could have been lost due to the recession. It was our privilege to help.

My Journal, July 3, 2009

We are approaching five months from the date of Tommy's accident, and there is still no real news on any recovery from the paralysis.

Robyn told me that in her prayer time she asked God whether the prediction made by the lady named Terry almost five months ago at Washington Regional was really true or not. She said the Bible verse that came into her head over and over again during that prayer was Matthew 11:8-9.

When she looked that verse up and read the paragraphs around it, Jesus is being asked, "Who is John the Baptist?" The answer includes the fact that John was a prophet. Robyn took this as God telling her that Terry was being prophetic as well when she told Tommy in his hospital room that he would walk again.

When Robyn was telling me all of this, I related to her that I had experienced a vivid dream recently of Tommy walking into a room full of people with braces on his legs. In addition, when I told Marshall about this dream, Marshall said he'd had the same dream three or four times over several months. It was the same dream Eddie Drilling communicated to me a few weeks after the accident.

REFLECTIONS: SEVEN YEARS LATER

By Robyn Van Zandt

The times when I would come home from Craig were a respite. The boys were there and that had its own issues, but I could go to a restaurant and eat when I wanted. I could rest when I wanted. I could visit with friends.

So while I wanted Tommy to come home, part of me was dreading him being home. I wanted him to be home for him. I wanted him to experience being home. But I didn't know what in the world it was going to be like. I was very anxious about life going forward.

More than anything, I wouldn't have the experts around me. I would be totally responsible for him. We had tried to get a team of doctors, but we were still educating the doctors, because Tommy's condition wasn't a common thing. They hadn't dealt with this kind of a situation.

In Colorado, I felt pressure to learn everything in a short amount of time, which was my choice. I was doing my best to consider all the equipment he would need, including the van, learning how to dress him, bathe him, change a catheter, change a trach, respond in emergency situations, drive and maintain an electric wheelchair. ... It was extremely stressful trying to get him up and ready in time to

make it to his classes in the morning. I had to leave
the room several times to cry or get myself together.

Chapter 9

Rocky Mountain Adventures

*The L*ORD *will guide you always; he will satisfy your needs in a sun-scorched land and will strengthen your frame. You will be like a well-watered garden, like a spring whose waters never fail.*
ISAIAH 58:11 (NIV)

When Tommy first went to Denver, I expected to spend a great deal of time out there with him. As it turned out, that wasn't the case.

Tommy was blessed with visitors every weekend, and Robyn spent every other week in Denver, so he had experienced little loneliness.

In fact, as summer marched on, Tommy asked Paul James, our friend who had been his "trip scheduler," for friends not to fill his remaining two open weekends. Most of the visits were two days of intense discussion for Tommy, and they were tiring to him. In addition, Tommy's physical therapy and educational sessions were intensifying as he prepared to come home in August.

So when Vicki and I flew to Denver in early July, it was just my third trip to see Tommy. And it was the first for Vicki, who had been busy as the "backup mom" in Fayetteville while Robyn was in Denver.

We scheduled our visit to coincide with taking Jack to Deer Hill Camp near Durango, Colorado. Jack flew to Denver on July 6, and Vicki and I followed on July 7. Robyn and Ross were already in Denver for the start of two weeks of training on how to take care of Tommy at home.

The timing had grown in significance because the surgery to implant a pacemaker-like device to stimulate Tommy's phrenic nerves was scheduled for July 8. We were thrilled the surgery could finally take place and that all of us could be there to support Tommy. We also were hopeful the surgery would help him wean off the ventilator before coming home.

That first night, Vicki had a bout of altitude sickness. The rest of us took Tommy to dinner.

The outing included two nurses, one of whom drove the huge van. It was quite a production to get Tommy in and out of the van, then into the restaurant. A nurse had to tilt the wheelchair backward every fifteen minutes for a "weight shift." With all of the batteries, tubes, and ventilator equipment, it seemed the nurses were busy most of the time.

Robyn had described an earlier dining-out experience as "not relaxing," and I now had a better understanding of what she meant. Still, we generally had a good time and we met our two bigger goals: Getting Tommy out of the hospital into a "semi normal" setting and having an early celebration of Tommy's fifthieth birthday, which was coming up on July 24.

OFF PACE

We were warned the surgery was questionable because Tommy had a low-grade infection in his lungs. Sure enough, even though he had to skip breakfast and was wheeled over to Swedish Hospital around 10:00 a.m. for surgery prep, the surgery was delayed at the last minute.

The surgeon was ready, but the infectious disease doctor did not want any foreign objects (the wires for the pacemaker that were to be attached to the phrenic nerves) introduced into Tommy while he had an infection of any kind.

Since we had prayed for guidance on this decision, we accepted the outcome, even though all of us were disappointed (especially Tommy) not to move forward. In one of the understatements of the year, Tommy said he was "tired of being on this ventilator."

With the surgery postponed, we looked for ways to enjoy the rest of the day. We started by going to an antique auto show right outside the hospital. Tommy was very hungry by the time we got him downstairs, and thankfully they were serving lunch.

Robyn fixed him a plate of food, but he had me prepare a second plate. I was happy to do it. Robyn had put barbecue on the plate she had prepared, while he bossed me to dress up a hot dog for him. This reminded me of something Big Dad would do after he was wheelchair-bound. I took it as an effort by Tommy to assert some kind of control in a new life where he had little.

Man, he enjoyed that hot dog, chased by a huge chocolate chip cookie!

That afternoon, Tommy and I went with his nurse to the gym on the first floor to hear motivational speaker Jason Regier, an accomplished athlete who wanted to be a professional soccer player before an injury left him as a quadriplegic.

Jason, a former patient at Craig, had been a part of a

gold medal team playing "quad" rugby at the 2008 Olympics in Beijing. His theme was persistence, and he talked about "taking one step forward." Several times he talked about the frustration of feeling like he had lost 9,900 of the 10,000 things he could do before he got hurt. Eventually he realized he had to make do and excel at the things he had left. His motto was "Do what you can, where you are, with what you have left."

Afterward, I asked Tommy how he felt when listening to Jason. His answer surprised me. I expected him to say it pumped him up to hear this strong motivational presentation. Instead, he pointed out that Jason had some use of a bicep that enabled him to roll a wheelchair. It wasn't until he came to Craig and saw people with various injuries "zipping around in a wheelchair" that Tommy realized he had a more serious injury. He didn't say any of this as if he were feeling sorry for himself; it was more like an observation he made to answer my question.

FINDING EMPATHY

Vicki and I arrived at Craig about 8:30 the next morning and found Robyn quietly sobbing as she stood next to Tommy in his bed. Tommy was running a low-grade fever and had a very upset stomach. He felt terrible, and this made Robyn emotional. She felt so sorry for him.

After a few minutes, she tried to be positive by saying how thankful she was that the surgery had been postponed. If it had been done as scheduled, she pointed out, Tommy would have been even more miserable. The nurses gave Tommy something for the nausea, and fortunately he felt better by early afternoon.

Robyn and I had a meeting later that morning with Fred Frech, who was in charge of helping families deal with the business issues of returning home. Like many of the administrative people working at Craig, Fred was a former patient himself and a quadriplegic. He was injured in a car wreck on the day of his high school graduation. He "hadn't even made it to the graduation party yet."

Robyn's questions revolved around trying to arrange for home nursing care and the cost to pay for it. Fred explained that most patients at Craig who needed a lot of home nursing care had to find a way for Medicaid to pay for it, but he wasn't able to tell us how to wade through the government bureaucracy to understand the benefits or if we could qualify.

My questions were about arranging Tommy's flight home. Fred said it was possible to fly on commercial airlines, with a first-class ticket for more room, accompanied by a nurse and a respiratory therapist. Our friend Neal Pendergraft had offered the use of his plane if it could meet all of the medical requirements. So Fred agreed to work with us to evaluate whether a private flight could accommodate our needs.

Fred looked at us as the meeting ended and said, "It ain't fair to have to deal with insurance, home modifications, travel, home health care, and money at the same time you are dealing with this kind of injury." The empathy coming from someone in Fred's physical condition carried a lot of weight with me.

DEER HILL CAMP DISTRACTIONS

Vicki, Jack, and I said goodbye to the rest of the family that afternoon and drove off toward Deer Hill Camp. The 340-mile drive from Denver to Durango is supposed to take seven hours, but we managed to make it in ten.

We drove part of the way and spent the night, and Jack

asked if we could take a "fun hike" the next morning. Vicki interpreted that as a last-ditch effort to break in his new hiking boots bought weeks before. He had been warned by everyone to break them in and claimed he had done so by walking once to the tree in his backyard.

We finally made it to Deer Hill about six o'clock that night. Jack immediately jumped into the spaghetti line for dinner with the rest of the campers, while Vicki and I sneaked off with the owners, our friends Beverly and Doug Copeland, to enjoy a glass of wine.

After dinner, Jack followed us to the car to unload his duffle bag. I walked with Doug, so I could not hear what Jack was telling Vicki. Later, she said he was telling her about his hiking group. He said they were all weirdos, and all of the girls were from small towns in the mountains (as if that were a bad thing).

Vicki didn't know if he was being serious or pulling her leg. Either way, I was glad we had told him that one of the goals at Deer Hill is to learn how to positively deal with people who aren't like you and still be a good teammate.

Jack returned from camp two weeks later full of good stories. It was clearly a positive experience and a confidence booster.

AN UPHILL CLIMB

After dropping Jack at Deer Hill, Vicki and I spent some much-needed time alone in Telluride, Colorado, then enjoyed a few days in Vail with Marsha and Rainer Twiford. While they didn't know Tommy, they wanted to support us, and we appreciated them traveling from Birmingham, Alabama, to be with us. Our visit was both therapeutic and fun.

We came back through Denver on July 17 for another

visit with Tommy, Robyn, and Ross. That night, we all took Tommy out for another birthday dinner. (I later joked that we were getting tired of his birthday.)

The rule at Craig is that if the patient can drive himself in his wheelchair to dinner, then a nurse is not required to go. We decided to "go it on our own" to Undici, another Italian restaurant that was nearby.

The trek turned into quite an adventure, with Tommy directing his wheelchair via a small cork toggle switch maneuvered by his chin. Over short distances this was not a problem, but over three blocks separated by curbs, it became a bit of a marathon. Each uneven crack in the sidewalk jammed the cork into his chin, but he winced and kept going. We laughed as he made his way slowly down the sidewalk.

At one point, we realized a curb cut across the street was forty feet uphill from us. Then we learned Tommy's electric wheelchair did not have enough power to go up that hill. So, while Ross held back traffic, we put the wheelchair on "manual" and I pushed it up the hill.

Nobody had told me the wheelchair weighed 350 pounds by itself; with Tommy's body weight, the whole contraption weighed 510 pounds. I pushed and strained red-faced as we slowly worked our way across, with the girls and Tommy laughing hilariously. In my stress, I called Tommy a "lard ass," which tickled us even more.

Looking back, it all sounds a little crazy now, even attempting to go to dinner on our own, without a nurse. Tommy had barely practiced driving with his chair, and he was really bad at it. And he was still so sick. Yet, we all wanted to try it. And we laughed the whole time at the absurdity of the adventure. There would be many more "cracks in the sidewalk" coming up for us in the days and weeks ahead.

The willingness to attempt new challenges, coupled with a strong sense of humor, would serve us well.

PACER, PART II

The surgery to insert the pacemaker finally was performed on Tuesday, July 21. After all of the buildup, and then the delay, it seemed everyone was at a fever pitch for this to happen. It was hard to concentrate on anything else, especially with so many people calling for updates.

The two-hour surgery went well, and less than ninety minutes after entering the recovery room, the staff was pushing Tommy to try out the new device. They would turn on the electronic pacer at the same time they dialed back the ventilator. This allowed them to see how much Tommy could breathe using only the pacer.

The first test he lasted five minutes, the next fifteen minutes, and the last one forty-five minutes. Tommy said it was very hard work, and he expressed some disappointment that he couldn't do more. He remembered a patient who got four hours off the ventilator only one day after surgery. Yet, the staff seemed pleased with his progress, so he was OK with it, too. In the big picture, all of us had to remind ourselves to be patient and to thank God that he could have the surgery at all.

Three days later, Tommy celebrated his fiftieth birthday —this time on the actual date of his birth.

Vicki had arranged for balloons and a cake (decorated with a Razorback). The nurses decorated Tommy's wheelchair, and they all came in and kissed him on the head. Brian Shaw gathered messages from friends into a very clever electronic birthday card that he delivered to Tommy in person in Denver. And Robyn and Ross hosted a

Skype party at the house in Fayetteville so people could all talk to Tommy over the computer.

My Journal, July 29, 2009

Tommy returned my call from last night. We have an understanding that I call his cell when I want to talk, and then hang up without leaving a voice mail because he needs a lot of help to listen to those. He can then see that I have called via Caller ID when someone activates his BlackBerry. He calls me back when he has time. I told him to wait to call until it is convenient for him. If I needed him urgently, I told him I would call twice in quick succession.

He said his efforts to get off the ventilator were going OK. He was able to do three hours of "weaning" on Sunday; however, he learned later that the ventilator was not totally turned off. It had been dialed down to provide less breathing support. Yesterday (Tuesday), when it had been turned totally off, he was only able to do twenty minutes.

He sounded disappointed, but not as if he was feeling sorry for himself. Mainly it was a matter-of-fact explanation of what was happening. He also said he felt no pain from working at it, but his body clearly was working very hard to breathe. He became exhausted and he mostly slept for twenty-four hours on Monday. The nurses, as well as another patient next door, told him that this was a common reaction.

I tried to encourage him by noting he had been in surgery only one week before. He also let me know on the call that Craig had moved his scheduled discharge date to the 27th of August (rather than the 13th). We agreed it was good to have more time to work on the weaning process.

At the end of the call I asked if he had ever bought the long-term care insurance policy we had discussed months prior to his accident. At that time, he told me he was going to buy it based on what he had learned from Big Dad's long illness. He replied that he had not, and I quickly moved on.

I didn't blame Tommy for not buying this insurance. I had not bought any, either. He had no clue that on this very day I had spent a good part of the afternoon with an attorney who specializes in Social Security, Medicaid, and Medicare issues. I was worried about the huge costs of taking care of Tommy at home, but Tommy didn't need me to put that concern on him right now.

Earlier that day, I had spent a couple of hours gathering financial information about the Van Zandt family for a questionnaire the attorney required for his initial ninety-minute consultation.

The attorney said the Social Security check for \$2,700 for Tommy's monthly disability (which he had not yet received) was over the maximum allowable income (\$2,022) required to receive home health care help from Medicaid. Therefore, he could get no help with home care expenses.

I was incredulous. His government check from one source was negating the opportunity to qualify for a far more important program (Medicaid). The monthly home health care expenses would be far greater than \$2,700. We expected we would need two nurses to get Tommy out of bed in the morning, and two more to put him in bed at night. At that time, we thought this would be at least $4,000 to $5,000 per month, maybe far more. Later, we learned it was significantly more.

I asked dozens of questions to probe for solutions, but the attorney was not encouraging in any way, even though it was clear he felt bad for us. The only solution to pay for Tommy's care with Medicaid, he said, was to put him in a nursing home.

I went out to my car and sat for a few minutes in the parking lot after this meeting. I felt as if I had been kicked in the stomach. What would I tell Robyn or Vicki? They were in no condition to take this hard news. I prayed a prayer for help and guidance, and then I drove on to the office. I visited with Cindy in my office to get her insight, which also helped me to process my thoughts.

On the way home, I called Robyn as promised, but I was glad I got her voice mail and didn't have to tell her about the meeting. Later that night, I told Vicki what Tommy had said about his weaning exercises, the news about the delayed discharge, and, finally, what I had learned in my meeting with the attorney. Of course, she was very upset.

I told her it seemed our only good option was to try to raise money in the Van Zandt Family Trust to pay for the home health care expenses, while trying to help the family to live on the $5,700 per month total from the combination of Social Security and private disability income. It seemed to me that Vicki and I would have to take on the family debts (cars, house, second mortgage, etc.); they clearly had no ability to pay them back.

Vicki's reaction was that we had to find someone to help us navigate or circumvent the government bureaucracy.

Then she added, "Well, Tommy is just going to have to get well enough to go back to work."

Vicki and I don't often pray together unless we are really troubled. That night in bed, we prayed together for guidance, for Tommy's recovery, and for strength for the family. We closed with thanks to God for what He had already done to help us. We "gave it to God," and we went to sleep.

The next morning, I read Psalm 20 during my daily quiet time. These are the first two verses: "In times of trouble, may the LORD answer your cry. May the name of the God of Jacob keep you safe from all harm. May he send you help from his sanctuary and strengthen you from Jerusalem" (NLT).

I knew God was encouraging me.

That same day I received an e-mail from Eddie Drilling as I sat on an airplane waiting to take off for a business trip to Houston. It said, "Thinking of you this morning and everything you have on your shoulders and knowing God is going to take care of you and Vicki for everything y'all are doing."

Then it quoted Isaiah 58:7–11:

Is it not to share your food with the hungry and to provide the poor wanderer with shelter—when you see the naked, to clothe them, and not to turn away from your own flesh and blood? "Then your light will break forth like the dawn, and your healing will quickly appear; then your righteousness will go before you, and the glory of the LORD will be your rear guard. Then you will call, and the LORD will answer; you will cry for help, and he will say: Here am I.

If you do away with the yoke of oppression, with the

pointing finger and malicious talk, and if you spend yourselves in behalf of the hungry and satisfy the needs of the oppressed, then your light will rise in the darkness, and your night will become like the noonday. The LORD will guide you always; he will satisfy your needs in a sun-scorched land and will strengthen your frame. You will be like a well-watered garden, like a spring whose waters never fail. (NIV)

Shortly thereafter, I sent an e-mail to Vicki to tell her God was encouraging us through Eddie's note and Scripture. I felt uplifted and strengthened, as did she.

It seemed to me God was encouraging us to keep helping the family financially, whatever it took and for as long as we could. If we responded, He would take care of us.

He was easing my hand off the financial resources He had given us, getting our hearts ready to do more. Once I gave up worrying about what to do and let go of the grip on our finances, I felt at peace.

Reflections: Seven Years Later

By Tommy Van Zandt

They tried a lot of therapies to get my diaphragm to work again, but none of them were working for me and that was very frustrating.

There was hope that with this diaphragmatic pacer I could get up to eight hours a day off the vent. At that time, very few people in the US had this technology. I was a borderline candidate for it because of my neurological damage.

During a visit when the respiratory doctors and nurses were in my room, my doctor said, "If I were to bet that this would work on someone, it would be Tommy." That gave me a lot of confidence that, no matter what, I would be able to make it work. I think he said that based on my positive outlook and my inner strength.

It was very tiring, though. Basically, the therapy puts you in a position of not being able to breathe but having to work through those fears and push yourself physically as much as you could to try to progress a little bit each day or each couple of days.

I showed very little progress while I was still at Craig. But one of the angels who came to me after I came home was Betty Adkins. She was a respiratory nurse I first met while in the hospital in Fayetteville, and she offered to come to the house and work with me a few times a week on the pacer.

Chapter 10

Prepping for Home

I waited patiently for the LORD; he turned to me and heard my cry. He lifted me out of the slimy pit, out of the mud and mire; he set my feet on a rock and gave me a firm place to stand. He put a new song in my mouth, a hymn of praise to our God.
PSALM 40:1–3 (NIV)

Bud Cummins visited Tommy in Denver in early August, and, like most everyone who made that trip, he came away encouraged and inspired.

"His demonstration of faith, courage, etc., did a lot more for me than anything I did for him," Bud wrote in his e-mail report to the rest of us. "I have been working and traveling all summer, and I showed up exhausted and actually left feeling a lot better, physically and mentally. Tommy is obviously in a tough jam, but he couldn't be dealing with it better. It is something to see."

Bud also perceptively picked up on some "apprehension" in Tommy about the impact his homecoming would have on his family. And Bud realized Robyn, who was still going through training to learn to care for Tommy, also had reasons to be nervous about bringing Tommy home.

"It appears to me that this will likely be stressful for both of them (probably each one worrying about the other)," Bud wrote, "and we should say a prayer for them in that regard."

With his discharge scheduled for the end of the month, we often were focused on the details of the move. I appreciated Bud's reminder to call on God to help Tommy and Robyn—and all of us, really—through the emotional challenges.

And those challenges were all around us.

The first two weeks in August were some of our most difficult since Tommy got out of the ICU in Fayetteville. The whole house was a mess as they put the finishing touches on making it handicap accessible. We walked around on construction paper that protected the hardwood floors. Vicki greeted the workers daily in her robe, then spent her days storing books, rehanging pictures, moving furniture, and sorting through the boys' closets to help figure out what they needed for the start of another school semester.

I focused on restructuring the family's financial plan to reflect the new realities. Brian Shaw and I had reviewed the various real estate partnerships Tommy was involved in, which in the aggregate had a negative value for him. So, given his family's limited income, my first goal was to reduce their debt to a manageable level. For instance, we sold Tommy's truck and four-wheeler and took the "cash value" from their life insurance to pay down debt.

Debby Nye, an attorney in Fayetteville, was advising us on qualifying for Medicaid. She had held a high position for the Department of Human Services and was referred to us by Scott Gordon, chief operating officer of Arkansas Children's Hospital. We needed all the help we could get from Medicaid, especially when we learned Tommy would initially need one or two people to care for him twenty-four hours a day. At the time, the estimated cost was $14,000 to $15,000 per month, and that was just for nurses. It didn't include things like the ventilator rental or unreimbursed medications.

All of this was a huge time commitment for me on top of trying to run our normal business. Frankly, there were days when it made me very melancholy. But each time I got down, the Lord picked me up.

My Journal, August 10, 2009

Yesterday, Vicki and I went with the boys to the contemporary service of Central United Methodist Church. The sermon by Senior Pastor Tony Holifield was titled "When You Are Distressed." The Scripture reference was Psalm 27:14, which can be summarized as follows:

- Wait on the Lord
- Be of good courage, then
- God will strengthen your heart

I felt a personal connection to this message, and I am trusting in it.

As we left church, Robyn called to tell us Tommy had spent fourteen hours with the ventilator in a "dialed down" (not off) position. I told her to tell Tommy this was the only time in his life I could describe him as "a big weaner," which Jack and I thought was hilarious.

INTERVIEWING CAREGIVERS

Mud drove to Fayetteville and spent nearly four days interviewing potential nursing care providers to help take care of Tommy in his home. She was perfect for this because she had spent fifteen years finding people to help take care of Big Dad. The job invigorated her because she knew she was the best one to do it. It also gave her something tangible to do after six months of feeling helpless. She told us the number of qualified candidates was much deeper in Fayetteville than in the Little Rock area, even though Northwest Arkansas has half the population.

My Journal, August 13, 2009

This week, as I packed my clothes to come to Little Rock for the last time before Tommy comes home, I became sentimental about our relationships with Jack and Ross. For more than six months, Vicki and I have been surrogate parents whenever Robyn has been in Denver with Tommy. We are so proud of them. We love them in a deeper, special way.

We have seen Jack grow into a more self-confident, considerate young man. The crisis of the accident, the visits to see his dad in Denver, the interaction with all of our family, and Deer Hill Camp have all contributed to this change.

We have had special times together, including last week. Ross, Jack, and I shot my new compound bow in the backyard and laughed about the idea of having Jack dress up like a deer so we could practice on him.

When I went out Monday and bought the family a new charcoal grill, we made a big production out of training Jack on how to cook on it for his mom and dad when they came home. Jack's food of choice is steak, so Vicki bought some big ones that he and I prepared on the new grill. I told him he was the *sous chef*, while I was the head chef. I teased him that he was now in training to observe my every move—from building the fire, to spreading charcoals, to seasoning the steak, to cooking it. Jack was relieved when we couldn't find aprons. "Aren't you taking this a little too far, Uncle Mark?" he said. Imagine the pride I felt two nights later when he called to let me know he and Ross were grilling chicken for dinner.

On my last night in Fayetteville (August 10), Ross and I had a man-to-man talk. To make my point about the gravity of the meeting, I asked him where we could go that would serve beer to a seventeen-year-old. He feigned ignorance, so we went to Arsaga's, a local coffee shop.

He told me that every night since the accident he had dreamed of his dad walking. He walked with a limp and a look on his face that said, "What are you looking at and why are you surprised?" Ross was astonished when I told him Eddie Drilling and I both had had similar dreams of Tommy walking and Brian Shaw had dreamed of fishing with Tommy. He told me that in one particular dream Tommy was speaking to a big audience of people, just like in my dream.

I started the conversation with the definition of an "authentic man" that Ross had learned with his dad last summer at a program called Christ in the Tetons. Robert Lewis, a former pastor in Little Rock who wrote *Raising a Modern Day Knight*, leads the

weeklong father-son camp. Lewis says a biblical
man:

- Rejects passivity
- Accepts responsibility
- Leads courageously
- Expects God's greater reward

The gist of my conversation with Ross was
twofold:

First, he needed to fully comprehend the new
role he must play in the family, especially with
Robyn. I bragged on how unselfish and wonderful
his mother had been. I emphasized that her life
had been impacted in every way, and that now he
must honor and support her. She needed his help.
I challenged him to do things for her around the
house without being asked, just to show her the
respect she deserved. If he would lead, I said, Jack
would follow and do the same.

I had previously shown him how to change the
air conditioning filters and how to start the weed
eater. He confessed that chores like these had
always been a hassle; now that he looked at them as
helping to support his mother, it would be different.

Second, I told him he needed to focus on
building up his college entrance test scores. He
needed to take charge and manage his requests
for college scholarship support. Vicki and I would
support him with any guidance we could, but his
choices for college were either limited or enhanced
by him.

I told him there was very little money saved
for college. This was hard, of course, but I felt Ross

could take it. And he was accomplished enough in school to gain a scholarship if he set his mind to it. I told him he had time in this senior year to manage the application process, but he needed to start now rather than later when it would be too late.

The conversation seemed more pleasant at the time than it feels as I write this. On the way home, he thanked me and said my comments "were really well organized." This amazed and amused me. I had hoped for a more effusive response after all of my preparation. Instead, I got a dry critique like one would expect from an English teacher. I should have expected it from a teenage boy. I hugged him and told him I loved him.

ANOTHER DELAY

Tommy and I had a hard time catching up with each other in early August, but we made up for it with a forty-five-minute talk on Saturday, August 15.

Tommy had not felt well. In addition to the pacer implant, he had undergone surgery to insert a suprapubic catheter. The two surgeries had taken a toll on his body, and he had been experiencing spasms, headaches, and very high blood pressure.

"The high blood pressure kind of scared me," he said.

The physicians at Craig were trying various medications to stabilize his system, including morphine and OxyContin.

Because of these problems, Tommy consented to stay an additional week at Craig. His new departure date was September 3.

"I really didn't want to do it," he told me. "I miss y'all and the boys."

The weaning process was really hard work, he said. When they totally dialed the ventilator to "off," he could do fifteen to thirty minutes, but he would come close to passing out. He was still optimistic and working hard.

"It's going to take longer than we thought," he said. "It may be three months or six months, but I'll stay with it however long it takes."

We spent a lot of time talking about his family. I told him how well Vicki and I felt that Ross and Jack were doing. He was interested to hear about my "man-to-man" talk with Ross, and he laughed when I told him Ross had said my thoughts were "really well organized."

Vicki had told me a story about Jack, which I relayed to Tommy. One of Jack's assistant football coaches had called his group together to tell the boys he was dealing with a difficult medical condition and that "sometimes life throws you a curveball." Jack went up to the coach after the meeting and said, "I will pray for you every day." This made both Tommy and me get a little choked up over the phone.

At the conclusion of the call, Tommy was upbeat and strong, as evidenced by a few more quotes I jotted down:

- "I've got to get to where I can give everybody hugs for what they have done for us."
- "They think I'm Superman around here since I have the strongest voice they've ever heard on a cuff."
- "I think I'm going to turn a big corner the next couple of days and be a healthier guy because of the new medications."

MY A-FIB

One of the things that went on hold in the immediate aftermath of Tommy's injury was treatment for a medical issue of my own.

I had been dealing with a heart condition called atrail fibrillation for three years, and I had been scheduled for a heart ablation procedure in March. We had rescheduled it for August, and my plan was to delay it again since Tommy was still not home. But Vicki and our sons pushed me to get it done. It was not an urgent situation, but their negative reaction to my proposed second delay helped me understand how much they had been worried about it.

So Vicki and I flew to a Cleveland clinic on August 18, and I had the surgery there on August 20. We came back to Arkansas the next day and immediately went to our cabin on the Little Red River to recuperate.

Robyn visited by phone while I was there, and we had several upbeat conversations. In one, I could sense her pride in how she and Mud had assembled a team of five caregivers to take care of Tommy. She told me how she had hired them and given each a pep talk about teamwork. I thanked God for answering our many prayers for the right people to take care of Tommy at home.

She also told me the Spinal Cord Commission had been unresponsive to her questions about giving us financial help with the $54,000 van that Tommy needed. I urged her to try to "box them in" to give us answers, and I gave her some pointers on how to do it.

The very next day, Robyn called to say her persistence had paid off. She went to the commission office in person, only to hear again what they couldn't do to help. In exasperation and frustration, she broke down and cried right there, expressing her concerns about all of the delays and hurdles. Within fifteen minutes after she left, they called to say they could help with the "handicapped conversion" part of the van cost ($22,000) and maybe also with the special mattress ($6,800) Tommy needed for his bed at home.

This thrilled Robyn, of course, and it pleased me to hear the excitement in her voice. I told her to tell Tommy right away, because he would be so proud of her and also because nobody in the world appreciated a bargain like Tommy Van Zandt (he's very thrifty, to put it mildly).

While I was at the cabin, I picked up a copy of *Sports Illustrated* with a cover photo of Marc Buoniconti, a former college football player who was paralyzed while making a tackle. I peeled through it looking for optimism, knowing that this young man's tragic football injury had spurred a lot of donations toward spinal cord research.

Instead, the article outlined how he was still on a ventilator after twenty-four years. At forty-two, he still required twenty-four-hour nursing care at a cost of $500,000 per year. Although he was working hard to inspire others to contribute to research, he had little hope for himself.

After reading it, I hid it from Vicki, and, soon thereafter, I threw it away so she wouldn't read it.

A TOUGH MEETING

Robyn, Tommy, and I participated in a "Team Discharge Conference" on Tuesday, August 25. This was supposed to be our final meeting before the revised discharge date of September 3. I called in from the cabin, and it seemed unfair somehow that I got to sit on the front porch in a rocking chair in that beautiful place while Tommy was still stuck in the hospital in Denver.

This was another very tough meeting. Dr. Johansen (Dr. J) started by saying Tommy was battling both a urinary tract infection and pneumonia and was being given "the strongest antibiotics we have" intravenously to fight them.

He said Tommy had been experiencing hallucinations and "had not been with us at times." The full dose of antibiotics would not be completed until September 2, he said, and he wanted to ensure Tommy was stable and clear of infection for at least a week after that. So, to "set up Tommy for success" at home, Dr. J recommended that Tommy stay yet another week in Denver.

Tommy listened and finally agreed to this third delay in going home.

"Am I going to be like this with repeated complications for the rest of my life due to my condition?" Tommy said.

Dr. J sighed.

"It's a risky condition to have," he said. "I'd be lying to you if I said you won't have problems periodically at home. You may have to go to the hospital from time to time to address complications."

"I knew this meeting would be tough for you, Dr. J," Tommy said.

It occurred to me then (and now) how amazing it was that Tommy heard this hard news and yet was worrying about his doctor having to deliver it.

I tried to break the somber tone by telling Tommy he shouldn't worry about a week's delay since the Arkansas Razorbacks were playing a patsy (Missouri State) on the first weekend in September. Even with the delay, he could be home in time for the first real test with Georgia on September 19.

When the pulmonologist gave his report, he implied Tommy would be highly dependent on the ventilator for a long time. Robyn asked if Tommy would ever get off the ventilator and have his trach removed.

"We know of only one patient in the world in your condition who ever got off the ventilator full time and had the trach removed," the doctor said. "Your diaphragm is not stimulating well. An aggressive goal would now be to get off the vent twelve hours during the day and then get back on it at night."

"That's the first time we've heard that news," Tommy said. "It's a shock. Maybe our hopes were too strong. We were hoping to do better than most."

It seemed that with each team meeting with Dr. J and the medical team, we were being told, little by little and gently, more negative news about Tommy's long-term prognosis. Looking back, I wonder if his condition at that time dictated them telling us, or rather, if they gradually released this news to us because they knew we could only take so much at one time. Most of the rest of the call was a blur to me.

Toward the end of the call, one of the medical team members said, "Tommy and Robyn, you are both very strong. Robyn, you came in here with a lot of fear, but you are leaving with a lot of confidence, and we are proud of you. Your boys are unusual and mature beyond their years."

The medical team then presented a card from all of them as a going-away present.

"We've enjoyed the process and the people here," Tommy said. "If you have to spend (six) months in one room, this place is probably as good as any."

As I hung up, I thought about how to update Vicki and Mud, both of whom naturally always pushed to know the latest news. I was disappointed in the new delay, but I totally agreed with the decision. My overriding sadness was about the thought of Tommy staying on a ventilator, with all of its resulting complications and quality-of-life challenges, for the rest of his life. I told Vicki and Mud the goal now was to wean off the ventilator for twelve hours during the day, but

I could not tell them with total disclosure of the long-term prognosis. It was too much to bear. Besides, I was not giving up hope, and neither would Tommy.

Two days later, I wrote Tommy a letter to try to encourage and strengthen him. I reminded him of the story of Gideon, which had been on my heart a lot in recent weeks. God chose Gideon to lead the Israelites against a huge army. Yet God asked Gideon to pare his army of tens of thousands down to a mere three hundred men—just to prove the victory was God's, not Gideon's.

"What you accomplish from this point on will be God's victory and everyone is going to see it," I told Tommy in the letter. And I ended it by saying, "You continue to be an awesome testimony to the strength and courage that comes only from the Lord. And I know the Lord is very proud of you. 'The LORD does not look at the things people look at. People look at the outward appearance, but the LORD looks at the heart' (1 Samuel 16:7, NIV)."

STILL GRIEVING

A few days later, Vicki asked me to talk with Mud because she was very upset. Tommy had not been able to call her much for the previous two weeks because he had been so sick. Mud didn't know how really sick he had been (and neither did I until the team conference call), but her instincts were that he was "not doing well at all." I consoled her as best I could, pointing out that he was gradually getting better. But I acknowledged she was basically correct in her instincts.

The next day I asked her to join me on Saturday for a tour of our farms in the Arkansas Delta. She grew up in the Delta, so I knew this outing would bring back good memories of her childhood.

In the meantime, Vicki broke down and cried. She told

me she felt like a failure. She said she couldn't help her mother feel better, that she worried about Robyn, Jack, and Ross, and that all of her trying to help wasn't successful in helping any of them.

It was obvious all of this was really grief for Tommy and worry about the impact it had on the whole family. I told her so. We also talked about how all of us were still grieving, so she shouldn't take it so hard on herself to try to "fix" everyone. It was impossible to shortcut the grieving process.

That Saturday (August 29) was a beautiful day for a farm tour. I picked up Mud at 8:30 a.m., and we didn't make it home until about 3:30 or 4:00 p.m.

Our first stop was a new farm we had bought with our friends the Clarks and the Drillings. She "oohed" and "ahhed" over the little pecan grove. She got out and walked some newly plowed ground where we looked for wheat sowed by a crop dusting airplane. Then we were on to England, then to Stuttgart, and finally to our little farm near Crocketts Bluff on the White River.

Mud loved the renovated barn we were using as a hunting clubhouse. We rode on a Ranger four-wheeler all around the farm, and I showed her our newly prepared dove field and the duck hunting reservoir. She was very quiet as we rode, except for a few comments about how beautiful everything was. My guess is she was recalling all of those fond memories of the family farm back in Blytheville, and she told me she was thinking about her father, who loved the soil.

For lunch, we went to my favorite place in a "wide place in the road" in Ethel, Arkansas. There we had what she described as "the best cheeseburger I ever ate."

My friend Mary runs the place. As we were leaving,

Mary showed Mud the dollar bills tacked to the wall. They were signed by people from all over the country who had eaten there (mostly to hunt in the White River Refuge). By coincidence, Mud spotted a dollar signed by her grandson, Jack Van Zandt. Jack had signed it when I took him and Tommy to breakfast after a duck hunt back in mid-January, about two weeks before the accident. Of course, Mud loved seeing Jack's dollar in Ethel. And I have thought so many times about that last hunt with Tommy and Jack. That memory means everything to me.

Ups and Downs

That Friday, we celebrated Mud's seventy-sixth birthday with a party at our house. The whole affair was perfect since Marshall, Beth, John Mark, Melissa, and the Clarks were all there with us. To top it off, Tommy called from Denver right before dinner to tell Mud happy birthday. It was a beautiful night in every way, including the weather, so we could enjoy the celebration outdoors. All of us love Mud so much, so it gave us great joy to celebrate the happy occasion with her.

The preparations for Tommy's trip home weren't nearly so pleasant. Earlier that week we were informed that Craig Hospital had made a "policy decision" and wouldn't allow Tommy's nurses to fly home with him on a private aircraft. It was an insurance problem for the hospital, they said. Since the nurses had to be on the flight, we had to make a new plan to fly home on an air ambulance.

This infuriated me because we had spent eight to ten weeks working hard on the details of the private flight with our friend Neal Pendergraft, who had offered to pay for the cost. Representatives of Craig Hospital (Fred Frech and his team) had worked hard on these details, too. It seemed if this was going to come up, it should have been many weeks earlier. Otherwise, we should have been "grandfathered" and allowed to use the private plane.

Mainly, I was concerned we would offend Neal with this abrupt, last-minute change. Neal and his sweet wife, Gina, had also been working very hard planning a second Tommy's Nite Out fundraising event at their "barn" on their beautiful family compound in Fayetteville, so I was sensitive about that, as well. Fortunately, Neal was gracious and told me not to sweat it, and that private aircraft charters are canceled all the time.

This was the only occasion when Craig Hospital let us down, so in the big picture it was best to get over it quickly and move on.

My Journal, September 8, 2009

Tommy called to let us know his homecoming would be delayed until September 17 due to blood pressure problems. His blood pressure would spike to 165 or 187 over 90, then fall to as low as 75 over 45. He said Dr. J wanted to try to moderate these swings with medication, which would take time. Overall, Tommy was understanding about the delay.

LUNCH AND THANK YOU

On Friday, September 11, Robyn hosted a luncheon at the office of Crawford Construction to thank the contractors and subcontractors for their work on the Van Zandt home.

Afterward, I called Cody Crawford to ask him how it went. He said everyone loved it, and that both Robyn and Brian Shaw did an excellent job. He said he knew it would be very hard for Robyn, and that she broke down once but recovered quickly. Her words were meaningful to all of these generous men who had given so much to the job.

Cody told me that both Advanced Mechanical and Hill Electric had donated all of their time and materials. Other subcontractors were small and could not afford a total donation, but they may have donated labor or something else to the job. Those who were paid were paid by Crawford Construction, which also donated the generator ($6,000 to $7,000, in my estimation). All in all, the renovation would have cost more than $30,000. Cody wouldn't let us pay a penny. He said he didn't want a thing, but he was going to keep helping and keep watching because, "I know Tommy is going to do great things in the future."

My words of thanks seemed insignificant compared to the huge hearts of these men, especially Cody.

Reflections: Seven Years Later

By Tommy Van Zandt

I remember being very frustrated because I wanted to get home and start trying to work toward living a normal life—with my family, at work, with my friends. I was tired of being in a hospital and tired of being cold all the time with no control. There were a lot of prayers on my behalf. A lot of prayer warriors seeking God's help for healing me as soon as possible.

The other reason it was frustrating was because friends in Fayetteville had set a date for the Tommy's Nite Out. I really wanted to be there for that. My doctor and nurses all knew my sense of urgency, and they probably released me sooner than they wanted, which is probably why, after being home for a very short time, I was back in the hospital.

Chapter 11

Home at Last

*This is the day that the L*ORD* has made;*
let us rejoice and be glad in it.
PSALM 118:24 (ESV)

After all the delays and health setbacks, we continued to pray, hope, and prepare for Tommy's move home. And God continued to answer our prayers and provide just what we needed.

My Journal, September 12, 2009

Tommy called today while I was at our farm. He said he needed to "get over this last hurdle" of blood pressure fluctuations, and then he could come home.

"Other than that," he said, "I'm fit as a fiddle."

He expressed confidence that everything was going OK because Dr. J felt confident he was making progress. I wondered how difficult it would be for him at home without being in touch with Dr. J. After almost daily interaction for seven months, this would be quite an adjustment. I prayed that our new team of caregivers could fill this void.

God has brought us a team in answer to those prayers. One of them is Sherry Walt, who will be helping on weekends. She has two grown sons, so her experience with teenage boys will be invaluable with Ross and Jack. Sherry's husband was in an accident a few years ago, and he only lived two weeks before he died. She told Robyn she wanted to take care of Tommy the way she wished she could have cared for her husband if he had survived.

Two of Tommy's nurses in the ICU at Washington Regional have been following his progress while he's been in Denver. Betty Adkins, a respiratory therapist, and Stephanie Ryan, an ICU nurse, have both volunteered to help Tommy for free in their off time from work. This is an incredible, totally unexpected blessing.

Jill Hollis heard about another nurse who just moved into the neighborhood (a male married to an internal medicine doctor). When Robyn called him to introduce herself and to see if he might check on Tommy in the event of an emergency, he too volunteered his time. He said he had been blessed and he would be happy to do it as long as she wouldn't pay him.

The Lord has brought us the team to care for Tommy at home, far beyond our wildest expectations.

Welcome Home!

Tommy finally came home on Thursday, September 17—seven months and ten days after his accident. The air ambulance landed at Drake Field in Fayetteville around 11:30 a.m. And when the two nurses who had accompanied him from Craig Hospital sat Tommy up in his wheelchair, he promptly passed out.

"If they got you up at 6:00 a.m., wouldn't let you have a bite to eat until noon, then filled you full of drugs and laid you in a little plane for three hours, wouldn't you pass out?" he told me later that day. "I'm fine now!"

Tommy made the driver go by Razorback Stadium on his way home so the nurses could admire it with him. It was "a longer but prettier route," he said, and he wanted the nurses to go back to Denver with a good impression of this place that he loves so much.

Tommy's return had been scheduled and rescheduled so many times it was hard to keep count. And when he finally did return to Arkansas, his flight was late arriving. Still, when they made it to the Van Zandt home, twenty-five or thirty special friends who had braved all of the delays stood in the rain to welcome Tommy back.

The two nurses, Greg and Trish, helped Tommy settle in and then trained the five local caregivers on how to deal with the vent, trach, and cuff. Trish took lots of pictures to show the staff at Craig, and she cried when they left the next day.

My Journal, September 18, 2009

Vicki, Mud, and I got to join the family and caregivers for dinner. Jack and I cooked hamburgers on the new grill, complete with hickory chips for flavor. It was a beautiful, joyous night, because we were together and Tommy was home. I fed Tommy his hamburger, and he bragged on that burger with every bite. Afterward, I asked him how his first day at home had been.

"I feel like I'm in a wonderful dream," he said, "like in *The Wizard of Oz.*"

We talked about how good our friends had been to us, and how strong and close our family had become.

"Don't you wish everyone was as blessed as us?" he said.

Earlier that day, I was using Tommy's desk at work for what I hoped would be one of the last times. As I opened a drawer looking for a pair of scissors, I found a copy of a three-page letter Tommy had handwritten to Marshall on Marshall's twenty-first birthday. It touched me because it reminded me about how much Tommy had helped us raise our sons. Perhaps the most poignant paragraph was one that talked about dealing with tough times.

"There will be failures, bad decisions, and just plain bad luck," Tommy told Marshall. "You will have doubts from time to time. Remember this above all else ... God is with you always. This is a marathon, not a sprint ... Use Him! It is the most important relationship you will ever have."

As I left his office, I made sure nothing was on the top of his desk—it was perfectly clean. Tommy and I agreed that this was better than putting all of the stuff back as he had left it eight months before.

Coming back to a clean, fresh start was the way it needed to be for him.

COMPLICATIONS

Six days after Tommy came home, I got a sickening call from Robyn. Tommy was in the Fayetteville hospital with a urinary tract infection and a fever of 105 degrees. We tried to take this in stride. We knew complications were bound to occur, and we were optimistic the infection would clear up quickly. As each day led to another, however, the staff at Washington Regional continued to treat him, run tests, and keep him in the hospital.

That Monday, Robyn called requesting prayers because Tommy had a staph infection in his lungs. She didn't have many details, but promised to call me back when she knew more so I could update Mud and Vicki.

While I waited for her to call back with more information, Vicki called me. She had been with Mud all day. It was the second anniversary of Big Dad's death, and Vicki said Mud seemed to be "near the end of her rope." Mud thought she should sell her house and move to an apartment in Fayetteville so she could know what was going on up there. She was frustrated at not being able to call Tommy and didn't want to burden Robyn with calls when she was already swamped trying to help Tommy and the boys. Vicki felt she needed to go to Fayetteville herself to help Robyn. Overall, I felt very sad and helpless. I prayed to God and asked for His help. I told Him I was taking His hand, and we really needed His help.

I was at the office the next morning when Robyn called to say Tommy was getting worse. He was lethargic and hardly responsive. She sobbed as she asked me to drive to Fayetteville to help evaluate if he was getting the right medications. She knew I would press for details on his condition from the staff in the hospital. She always focused more on how Tommy felt and looked and acted.

I dropped everything, ran home to pack an overnight bag, and was on the road in an hour. During the drive, I got a call from Robyn's brother, Doug Sims. Doug, a radiologist in Dallas, had read on the blog that Tommy had an infection, and he wanted to know more details. Unfortunately, I didn't have any, but I promised to call him back as soon as I did.

When I arrived at Washington Regional around 1:30 p.m., Tommy's fever had subsided and he was perfectly coherent. The nurse on duty said he was "200 percent better" than he had been at 6:45 a.m. when she had started her shift.

By 2:30 p.m., I knew Tommy had three infections (MRSA, Enterobactor cloacae, and Stenotrophomonas maltophilia)—one of which was the staph infection in his lungs. They were giving him six high-powered drugs by IV—Zyrox, Zosyn, Doxy, Tobra, Levaquin, and Bactrim. When I passed this information along to Doug, he said he thought the treatment sounded good. This made me feel much better, and I immediately called Vicki so she would know and could call Mud.

As Tommy ate pudding and other snacks to strengthen him, he told me about how well Robyn had been doing at home with the caregivers. Her training in Denver had given her confidence, and she was teaching the new team what she had learned so he would get the best care. He also told me about the letters he had been receiving from some of his caregivers (now friends) at Craig Hospital. Specifically, he talked about letters from Tiffany and Cindy. It was obvious these letters meant a lot to him. He described these people in great detail, including their background, family life, and his previous discussions with them about faith. It seemed that faith was a common thread in all of Tommy's observations about people since the accident.

We talked for more than four hours, and then Tommy urged me to go home. He knew I was scheduled to host a program for about one hundred men early the next morning in Little Rock. He said he was "fine" and on the mend. So I left, and I got back to Little Rock about 9:00 p.m. Then I got up at 4:45 the next morning to get ready for the program.

DIALED IN

Tommy finished his antibiotics on October 8, and he was feeling well enough to take part in a video conference that day with the team at Sage.

The purpose of the meeting was to update each other on our progress toward our individual or company goals. When Tommy dialed in, I carefully watched our younger guys—T.J. Lefler, David Erstine, and Marshall. Brian and I, and to some extent Marshall, had seen and talked with Tommy a lot during his time in Denver, but T.J. and David had not seen him at all for eight months.

T.J. looked amazed and asked how Tommy moved his wheelchair. All of them were wide-eyed and focused on Tommy, often elaborating on details to enable him to catch up after being away from the office for so long.

Tommy congratulated them on doing a good job while he was out. He explained that he would be more involved in a week or two after he "worked out some vent issues."

"I want to be on top of my game before I come back to the office," he said. "I can create a lot of business, but I will need you guys to help me work it. They'll be team deals. I think we will be very successful."

TOMMY'S NITE OUT, PART II

The first huge Tommy's Nite Out party in Fayetteville was the night after our conference call. In fact, during the call Tommy had joked that "the first one at the party tomorrow night is to park by a bush and save it for me so we can empty my leg bag by it."

The theme, logo, and overall party concept was patterned after the wonderful Tommy's Nite Out in Dallas. Dozens of volunteers, led by Tony and Mary Beth Sherman, had worked for months to prepare for the event, the first of several annual fundraisers led by Tony and Mary Beth. We can never thank them enough for what they have done for the Van Zandt family for many years.

Vicki and I had driven to Fayetteville the day before the party so I could participate in the Sage team meeting in person, and also so we could attend Jack's ninth-grade football game. About the time the game started, the forecasted heavy rains came into the area—about six inches of rain between 7:00 p.m. Thursday and 11:00 a.m. Friday, the day of the party. After months of preparation for a party that was largely to be held outside in tents, we were thankful when the rain finally quit.

Neal and Gina Pendergraft's home and "barn" feels like it's in the country, even though it is in the middle of Fayetteville. More than a thousand tickets had been sold, so we wondered how many people would show up to park in a soggy pasture after the storm. They came in droves, more than nine hundred, according to the security team's "clickers." As the huge line of cars stacked up to enter, it looked like the night scene at the end of the movie *Field of Dreams.*

Robyn and Tommy arrived in the new van equipped to handle the wheelchair, purchased that very afternoon. Tommy had insisted on coming, even though he'd just finished the antibiotics the day before.

The newspapers were full of warnings about H1N1, or the "Swine Flu Virus," so we had reason to be concerned. Mud or a caregiver stood next to Tommy all night, holding a bottle of hand sanitizer. We positioned Tommy in the barn, and immediately a line formed to greet him. It looked like the Pope was in town. For nearly three hours, Tommy greeted and loved on every one of them. I guessed that he got to speak to at least three hundred people in person.

There was a fabulous silent auction, then a live auction led by our friend Doug Stovesand, and then the band (the Cate Brothers) played.

It was at this first Fayetteville Tommy's Nite Out that I met Walter Hixon, another one of "Tommy's Angels," and his beautiful girlfriend, Melissa.

Walter, a fraternity brother who had lived in the house with Tommy during college, has a large and successful family business. It turns out that Walter had always had a special affinity for Tommy, who had befriended him as a new pledge.

Walter bid on every expensive item in the live auction. He was bidding it up to raise more money for the family trust. At times, it seemed he was almost trying to bid against himself. In this and subsequent Tommy's Nite Out events, Walter spent tens of thousands of dollars each time to help the Van Zandt Family Trust. And he inspired others to give, too. We will never forget Walter's generosity.

The party was fabulous in every way. Many of Tommy's fraternity brothers came to see him, so it was a reunion for them. Family and friends came from all around, representing not only different cities but various stages of life for all of our extended family. In that regard, it felt like a wedding. The tone was upbeat and fun.

During the party, Robyn delivered a message of thanks that moved and motivated everyone.

Robyn's Message at Tommy's Nite Out, October 9, 2009
I wanted to take this opportunity on behalf of our entire family to thank all of you for supporting us over the last eight months.

As you can imagine, our entire world has been turned upside down. In a matter of seconds, my healthy husband was paralyzed from the neck down. Earth-shaking, mind-blowing, heart-pumping, yet spiritually invigorating. There is no possible way I can explain my experience of the last eight months in a few short minutes, but it has been harder than and more blessed than you can possibly imagine.

From the moment Tommy fell, he began praying. The moment I got in the ambulance, I began praying. When our neighbors saw the ambulance, they began praying. And the praying hasn't stopped. It has not stopped, and it is what sustains us to this day.

Not only have your prayers sustained us, but your willingness to step forward and help us in very real and meaningful ways has been invaluable.

As most of you know, Tommy grew up in Arkansas, and from the day I met him he did not stop bragging about Arkansas. Being from Mississippi, I thought, *What in the world is the big deal?* But then I met his family and fell in love with them. Soon after, I began meeting his Arkansas friends in Dallas. Great people. Then we began visiting Northwest Arkansas. I, too, fell in love with Arkansas' beauty and the people. We made the big leap of faith and moved here in the summer of 2000. We have not looked back since.

We still love our friends in Dallas, and thoroughly enjoy visiting, but Arkansas is home. This community has turned out tremendously for us during this difficult time. The spirit of love, friendship, concern, and support is real, and it sustains our hope for the future. We will never be able to properly thank you for the impact you have had on us. We just hope to pay it forward someday.

I have always considered Tommy a gift and a special man. It occurred to me one day, he is not just meant for me and our family. A gift this good is meant to be shared. Thank you for sharing our lives with us. May God bless you, as you have blessed us.

We love you, and, believe it or not, this Longhorn is proud to say Go Hogs!!!!!

The response to the request for sponsorships was overwhelming, as was the generous response to auction items. Aaron Clark, who is the same age as our son John Mark and is a surrogate son of ours, even wanted to donate a baseball that his long-deceased grandfather had given him. Fortunately, his mother talked him out of it by saying his grandfather would probably prefer for Aaron's son (not yet born) to have it. Did I mention the ball was autographed by Babe Ruth?

The next night, Tommy told me about a conversation he had with my dad, who was eighty-five at the time and who had waited in the long line to greet him. Tommy has known Dad most of his life. We have all spent Thanksgiving and other family holidays together for many years.

"Dr. Saviers, I want you to take me fishing in three years," Tommy told him.

That stopped Dad cold. Then his eyes widened and he said, "OK, I will!" And he meant it.

Tommy had a hard time getting the comments out because he became so emotional. I didn't quite know what to say. It was the first time I had seen Tommy break down like this. I told him later that I wondered if Dad was more shocked to think about Tommy fishing or to think about being able to take Tommy in three years.

The emotions of so many friends supporting him and his family touched Tommy deeply. To me, it was very much like the story in the Bible where the paralyzed man is lowered by friends through the roof of a house so that he could be healed by Jesus.

"We can't overstate all of our blessings," Tommy said.

As Tommy had predicted, a lot of publicity came from the event. The regional edition of the *Arkansas Democrat-Gazette* ran an article and six pictures that took up more than a page of the society section that Sunday. We talked about how the event had created a "buzz" around town, and Tommy was searching inside about how to capitalize on it to do whatever the Lord had in mind for him to do. We agreed to pray about that together.

I told him not to worry about moving too fast, as the Lord would show us. Tommy responded by saying that perhaps these opportunities to speak out for the Lord would "help everything make more sense" of his injury.

WE NEED A QB

The next ten days went well. Buoyed by the party, settling in at home, and feeling better, Tommy came back to work. It took two people about four hours to get Tommy up, bathed, and fed each day. Three days the next week, he arrived about noon with one of his caregivers and stayed until five o'clock. And on October 18, he attended his church in Fayetteville for the first time since his injury.

We were feeling almost "back to normal" in our schedules, so it was depressing when Tommy was re-admitted to the hospital on October 20 with another infection. Robyn and the home care team had caught it earlier this time, so he didn't have to go by ambulance. He had a low-grade fever but said he felt fine. Robyn hoped he would be started on antibiotics and dismissed the next day.

Once in the hospital, however, Tommy went downhill fast. His blood pressure started spiking up and down. More tests were ordered, and Tommy and Robyn were very frustrated.

"Once they get their hands on him," Robyn said, "they seem to run all of the same tests again."

It came to a head on October 22, when Tommy went into respiratory arrest. The home caregiver called Robyn saying Tommy was having a very hard time breathing. Robyn immediately drove to the hospital and discovered that Betty (the respiratory therapist) had arrived just in time to literally save Tommy's life. The respiratory physician had not reviewed Tommy's medical records from Craig Hospital, had never treated a person in his condition, and thus had ordered his oxygen level dialed down to a level that would not support Tommy. Robyn later told me that Betty came in, recognized that "they were losing him," and started "throwing things around" to revive Tommy.

As Robyn recounted this story, she grew very angry, more than I had ever seen her. She had scolded the doctor, telling him that if he did not want to take Tommy as a patient and review his history (which Robyn had supplied to him), then he shouldn't have accepted the job in the first place.

I was proud of her for standing up to the doctor, and

we talked for a long time about how we could avoid this situation in the future. We needed a very tight medical team knowledgeable about Tommy, including a physician who specialized in respiratory care, one who specialized in infection, and a "quarterback." The quarterback for Big Dad had been Dr. Barry Baskin. He knew Big Dad's health history, and he always directed Mud about what to do with complications. We needed someone like him for Tommy.

Robyn and I agreed that we needed to consult with Dr. J in Denver and with Dr. Al Gordon in Fayetteville. Perhaps they could help us pick a team we could count on so we could avoid, whenever possible, the "grab bag" of physicians who knew nothing about Tommy's fragility and his history. We agreed to pray for the Lord to bring us this team, just as He brought us the home health care team.

COMMUNICATION QUESTIONS

Tommy was discharged on October 24, and it took him and Robyn several days to regroup and get back into any kind of routine.

During this time, there was quite a bit of discussion among those close to the family about communication. This was triggered by a brief e-mail I sent requesting that the planning group for Tommy's Nite Out in Fayetteville be the only ones who received the announcement of the final proceeds of the party—estimated at more than $400,000. This was so much more than we ever expected—a huge blessing!

The amount was fantastic, of course, but I was very concerned that some might conclude the family no longer needed financial help. I knew we were rapidly depleting the Van Zandt Family Trust after paying $32,000 for the van and spending $18,000 to $22,000 a month more than their income on home care, medications, the ventilator rental, and other expenses. In reality, the $400,000 would last about nineteen months before the family trust ran out of money again.

Also, immediately after the first Tommy's Nite Out in Dallas, the planning team announced more than $200,000 in net proceeds. Three months later, we were still trying to reconcile and collect all of the money. Some pledges were not honored or more expenses were incurred, and it appeared the net proceeds were more like $155,000. This was nobody's fault; it was just a reality of holding a large event and the lag time to reconcile all of the donations and costs.

In addition, I had experienced some surprising reactions to what had seemed like harmless mass communication. For example, if the blog discussed a potential medical condition, then some people concluded Tommy must certainly have it. Another time, I was thoroughly questioned by a well-intentioned potential donor (after he had approached me to offer help): "Is the family moving into a smaller house? If not, why not? Is Robyn going to get a job? If not, why not? How long should we be expected to help provide financial support?"

These questions upset me, but also educated me in the reality that most people could have no clue as to what the family (especially Robyn) was going through or how deep the financial burdens had become. It was the negative side of having so many people involved in Tommy's situation. Most of the time, the communication had been positive and helpful, but I was trying to learn how to avoid the negatives. And I was trying to protect the family.

Trey Hollis and David Roth disagreed with me as to how to communicate about the financial results of Tommy's

Nite Out. These guys are among the best people we know, so they were probably right. After a lot of e-mails back and forth, we agreed to a plan that was sensitive to my concerns, but also more forthcoming than my original proposal.

The result was really a refined message, crafted with input from several people, including Tommy, Robyn, and Ron Clark. It expressed our overwhelming gratitude, noted Tommy's desire to return to work, pointed out that the contributions were "enough at this time to last for several months to pay family expenses, including nursing care for Tommy," and asked for everyone to keep praying for the family and Tommy's caregivers.

REFLECTIONS: SEVEN YEARS LATER

By Tommy Van Zandt

I'll never forget the first Tommy's Nite Out in Fayetteville. It was very surreal. It was cold and raining, but people just kept coming in the door and coming in the door. They were actually waiting in line to talk to me, which I could not fathom.

They were my friends, but also people I did not know. And they actually wanted to talk to me. The first thing out of their mouths was almost always, "I've been praying for you." Then it was, "You look great." There were some tears on their part, but I was filled with joy, and I was filled with the Holy Spirit.

I remember everybody was worried about germs, worried about people touching me and getting too close. My mother sat there with a bottle of hand sanitizer making everyone clean their hands before they got near me, which was totally embarrassing.

I wanted to hug every single person so badly. I was and always have been a hugger. My condition doesn't allow for a good, full-on hug. It was frustrating. It's still frustrating. I hate it. I'm so full of love for everyone, and everyone is so full of love for me. The best way I know to show it is with a hug. And it's a compromised hug at best.

I told everyone early on to kiss me on my bald

head, and to this day many people still kiss me on the head when they see me—males as much as females. I have said "I love you" to so many guy's guys—guys who don't say that. I make it a point to say what I'm thinking. Now, most men who are around me will say that. But some of the men who are closest to me still won't kiss me on the head.

They rolled me out before I wanted to leave. I hadn't been able to talk to everyone. I was full of adrenaline and the Holy Spirit. I wanted to go all night. But they knew I was tired and needed to go rest, which was the right call.

Chapter 12

Sustaining Grace

I was given a thorn in my flesh, a messenger of Satan, to torment me. Three times I pleaded with the Lord to take it away from me. But he said to me, "My grace is sufficient for you, for my power is made perfect in weakness."
2 CORINTHIANS 12:7–9 (NIV)

Tommy showed signs of improvement as the calendar turned to November. He came to the office on several days. He went with Robyn to Jack's football game on November 5. He dictated e-mails for one of his nurses to type. And he joked with me that his goal was to get back to sending fifty e-mails per day.

Robyn was still working on finding the right "quarterback" for the physician team, and we were still praying for guidance. Meanwhile, she was growing more and more comfortable in her role of managing Tommy's care at home.

One night, the caregiver woke her up because Tommy's blood pressure had shot up to 200 over 100. Robyn immediately knew to sit Tommy upright to enable the pressure to subside. It was amazing to me that Robyn had learned to deal with Tommy's medical complications in such a short amount of time.

Our attempts to get Medicaid to pay for the home care staff, however, continued to move slowly. Debby Nye, the attorney helping us, was appealing a state regulation that limited assistance to only those living in a nursing home. It seemed ridiculous that this regulation existed in the first place, since clearly it would be less expensive for a patient to live at home than in a nursing home. We were excited to think our appeal might enable other patients to live at home.

We also were looking into options for Tommy's physical therapy. Dr. J in Denver had strongly recommended an FES bike for Tommy to ride to provide stimulus to his legs. Someone had sent me an article about another exercise technique where the patient "walked" erect on a machine.

I had encouraged Robyn to fully investigate these therapies. The trust was prepared to pay for them, and I did not want Robyn's concerns (or Tommy's) about money to stand in the way of progressive treatments.

My Journal, November 9, 2009

Tommy was able to go in person Saturday to watch his beloved Arkansas Razorbacks play South Carolina at the stadium in Fayetteville. It was a beautiful fall day—perfect football weather.

My thoughts turned back to Denver, reflecting on how Tommy had bragged so much on Arkansas and the Razorbacks to his friends on the health-care team there. And I also thought about him making the ambulance driver go by Razorback Stadium on the way home from Denver—just to show it off to his visitors from Craig Hospital.

It made me smile to think about how much Tommy would enjoy being at this game.

THE LIFE COMPASS

Tommy and I were talking by phone about a few business matters one day when I asked him how he was feeling.

"Well, I'm at the office, aren't I?" he said. "Been here all day. Doing great. I'm 100 percent, ready to rock and roll. I know I'm the luckiest brother-in-law in the world. Now, what can I do for you?"

I asked him to stay positive, to continue to contribute at the office, and to keep thinking outward on others rather than inward. I told him he was inspirational, so keep it up.

"I think we can do that," he said.

It was around this same time that I told Tommy about the "Life Compass" I was working on in a program called Men's Fraternity. Each of us in the program was creating a personal "compass" for ourselves consisting of dreams and goals that would be central for the rest of our lives. I told him one of my major goals was to help him and Robyn with their ministry. I told him I wanted to "carry his water" for him.

He seemed a little taken aback by this, but also very pleased. He promised to think and talk more about this idea.

Later on, when refining my goals, I added that I wanted to help write a book about the Van Zandt family journey, thinking maybe this would be a good way to broaden their ministry.

DUCKS AND TURKEYS

The opening day of duck season was November 21, and I was excited because both Marshall and John Mark would join me at Circle S, our duck club in southeast Arkansas. It was the first time for us to hunt together since we were in Argentina the day before Tommy was hurt.

When Marshall arrived from Fayetteville, he told me Tommy had another urinary infection—his third in the two months since coming home from Denver. Marshall said Tommy was very frustrated to have to go back to the hospital for testing and IV treatments.

When I called to check on him, Tommy said he was only at the hospital eight or nine hours that Friday. Dr. Gordon, Tommy's quarterback the first couple of years, had helped "spring him out" so that he could go home. It seemed our "dream team" of physicians (and treatments for infection) was taking hold and working to help keep him out of the hospital.

Robyn also told me Tommy had a "place" on the skin of his rear end that "we need to watch" to ensure it didn't turn into a wound. The nursing team was making Tommy stay in bed and was turning him from side to side, just as they had done months before. Robyn asked me to pray for this to heal so they could come to Thanksgiving dinner in Fort Smith (an hour van ride) on the next Thursday.

When I sent Tommy an e-mail the Tuesday before Thanksgiving to see how he was doing, here's how he responded: "Hey Mark ... I am feeling very well and am at the office. Janie and Robyn are making me come home at 2:00 p.m. to give my 'fanny' a rest. It is doing fine and I will be ready for Thanksgiving dinner on Thursday. See you there."

Tommy was right. His "fanny" was doing well enough for him to join us for Thanksgiving dinner. My sweet sister, Ann Appleton, and her husband, Dick, had graciously offered to host. For many years, Vicki and I had hosted Thanksgiving in Little Rock, but the three-hour ride from Fayetteville would have been very difficult for Tommy.

Dick had an elaborate ramp built so Tommy's wheelchair could come up some steep steps into the front door. This is just one example of how Dick and Ann have helped Tommy.

Ross and Jack joined us on "Thanksgiving eve" to enjoy the birthday party for our "November birthday crowd" (four family birthdays in November). It made us feel good that Jack and Ross wanted to come early to be with their extended family.

Robyn drove Tommy to Fort Smith on Thanksgiving Day, and they stayed about five hours. Tommy ate two full plates of food to match his customary intake. All in all, it was a wonderful day, for which we were all thankful.

Around six that evening, Jack and Dad and I loaded up my Tahoe to head to the duck woods of eastern Arkansas. Jack had grown to love hunting, so planning for this trip had helped sustain us in some of the tough months earlier in the year.

We drove about four-and-a-half hours to our farm in Saint Charles, Arkansas, the same place we stayed the previous January, right before Tommy was hurt.

Back then, Jack was slow-moving, especially very early in the morning when it was time to get ready for the hunt. Tommy almost had to wrestle him out of the shower, all while gathering up Jack's gear for him. So imagine my surprise on this trip when Jack knocked on my door at 5:00 a.m. to make sure I was awake. He then promptly fixed himself a bowl of cereal before loading his gear in my car, ready to go. What a difference ten months had made in terms of Jack's maturity and self-reliance.

My Journal, December 6, 2009

Tommy came to the office Tuesday for his second monthly "hot sheet" staff sales meeting. The team is becoming more accustomed to Tommy being back at the office and being more involved in the business.

Tommy used humor to put everyone at ease with his situation. One of the guys asked Tommy to comment on a conversation Tommy viewed as confidential. When pressed again to comment, Tommy said, "My trach went out," so he couldn't talk anymore.

When the conversation turned to a client who had been slow to pay his bill, Tommy said, "Roll me out in this wheelchair and maybe he'll feel sorry for us and pay."

Brian Shaw and I had a conversation on Friday about how Tommy was doing. Brian said Tommy's blood pressure had been dropping as low as in the 50s on some days. Tommy has learned to tilt his wheelchair way back every few minutes to help prevent this problem.

There was a training session for the Sage staff this week to show everyone what to do in the case of an emergency with Tommy. On one day that week, Tommy's nurse Jamie had told Brian that Tommy had kind of gone into a stupor for about thirty seconds while in the office.

All of this had led Brian to ask Tommy if he would prefer for the team to come to his house for meetings. When he brought it up, however, Tommy said, "I'd go to drinking heavily if I couldn't come to the office."

Today is Sunday, and this morning I flipped on the TV in the kitchen while preparing our morning coffee. Normally, I don't watch TV preachers, but the exception on this occasion was Charles Stanley.

His sermon on "Sustaining Grace" referenced 2 Corinthians 12:9, and it outlined God's answer to the apostle Paul's prayer for his own healing from some severe health issue. Dr. Stanley said God has any of four answers to our prayers: Yes, no, wait, and "My power is made perfect in weakness."

The fourth point, "My power is made perfect in weakness," was God's answer to the apostle Paul's prayer for healing. Dr. Stanley went on to lay out the seven reasons God may answer a prayer with the fourth option. They are:

(1) God, through grace, releases supernatural strength to believers.

(2) Grace ignites determination in us.

(3) Grace echoes in our spirit that God is with us.

(4) Grace keeps pointing us to God's goal (for the circumstance).

(5) Grace reminds us that God enables us to come through this trial in faith and in a deeper relationship with Him.

(6) Grace assures us that God has the situation in control.

(7) Grace awakens our faith that God will turn our tough times into something good.

Tears welled up in me because I couldn't help but apply this sermon to Tommy and to all of the thousands of prayers we had all offered to God asking for healing.

I cried by myself for a while. I did not want to believe God's plan was not to heal Tommy's paralysis. I did not give up hope for more healing, but I did realize God's grace was being made perfect in both Tommy and Robyn. We could all see evidence of God's supernatural strength, and His Holy Spirit, in each of them. And we had witnessed a lot of physical healing with Tommy—but not his paralysis.

JOLTED FROM NORMALCY

Tommy went back into the hospital on December 17 with another infection. This time, the doctors decided to remove the "PICC line" that had been used so many times to administer antibiotics, while inserting a "port" for the same purpose.

Hearing this news was hard because it jolted me out of the "normalcy" of a duck hunt with friends and into the worry of another infection in Tommy. As hard as we tried to get to "normal," clearly we now had a "new normal." These problems were not going away.

As always, I prayed for Tommy and Robyn and the boys, this time for not only healing, but also for strength to help them live with these discouraging setbacks. And I prayed for solutions to these continuing infections.

Inside, my deep concern was whether or not we could keep Tommy out of the hospital for any reasonable period of time.

Later that night, fellow duck club member and friend Mack Moore, a semi-retired urologist, asked about Tommy. When I told him Tommy was back in the hospital fighting another infection, Mack advised that Tommy should have his catheter removed to avoid a continuing stream of bacteria into his body via that foreign object. In lieu of a "full-time catheter, he should have intermittent catheterizations, maybe four to six times per day."

Mack was quite assertive, and it occurred to me that his advice might be another answer to our prayer for solutions to help Tommy avoid infections. I passed the advice on to both Tommy and Robyn, in part because I felt it offered hope for helping him stay out of the hospital.

My Journal, December 23, 2009

Pete Hoover, our friend and neighbor, died suddenly of a heart attack on Saturday. Of course, this shook us up, as it did so many of our mutual friends. We have lived across the street from Pete and Barbara for many years and watched their daughter grow into a fine woman (and friend). Pete's death was hard on us.

Today, after the funeral, I was attending the visitation and spent some time talking to some friends I had not seen in several years. One of them was very sweet and kind while expressing her sympathy to me and to our family about Tommy's accident. Yet her message really seemed aimed at how unfortunate Vicki and I must feel. It came across as sort of a "Job-like" question: "Why has this happened to us when we are good people?"

It dawned on me that her comments reflected

how many people feel when bad things happen to them. Yet this is not how we felt at all. I explained to her and her husband that we felt like God was helping all of us every day and that we were seeing miracles, even if those miracles were not everything for which we had prayed.

I told them we knew bad things happen to good people all the time. We were focusing on asking for and receiving God's help in our recovery, not questioning why this had happened to us.

RINGING IN A NEW YEAR

Vicki and I were preparing to leave for Dallas to attend a New Year's Eve wedding when Robyn called to say Tommy was back in the hospital with an infection in both lungs. His blood pressure had spiked way up, accompanied by really violent leg spasms—typical symptoms that come on when Tommy's body experiences problems he can't feel due to his paralysis.

This was the sixth time Tommy had gone into the hospital in less than four months. We initially expected that he would be treated and quickly released. But Robyn called the next day as we were driving to Dallas and said Tommy's blood pressure had dropped dramatically. He seemed sicker than he'd ever been, she said.

We offered to head to Fayetteville, but she told us to go on to the wedding and she would update us the next morning.

My prayer that night was different than usual, because inside I felt a special danger to Tommy. I asked Christ to encircle Tommy with protection and to please bring knowledgeable health-care workers to help him. A few days later, Robyn admitted she'd had virtually the same feeling. She was so concerned she had asked Jack and Ross to go see Tommy in the hospital on New Year's Eve "in case he didn't make it" through the night.

Tommy seemed better on New Year's Day, so we headed home to Little Rock. But that progress stalled, and on Monday, January 4, Robyn asked me to come to Fayetteville and to bring Mud.

Over the weekend, Mud had imploded emotionally. She had walked into our house on Sunday night with a zombie-like look on her face. She told us she had been driving in the neighborhood thinking about Tommy and had become confused as she wondered to herself, *Is this real what happened to Tommy?*

Vicki was concerned that she had experienced some kind of stroke. We gave her an aspirin and checked her blood pressure: 178 over 90. Vicki went to Mud's house to retrieve her blood pressure medicine. After an hour or two, she felt better and talked more coherently, but we insisted that she spend the night at our house.

She felt better physically the next day, but she was still anxious and now was expressing a lot of anger. She said she was mad because Robyn never called her to help or to really talk to her about Tommy. This gave us plenty to talk about during the drive to Fayetteville that Tuesday.

I had prayed about what to say and how best to say it. Mud and I drove together in one car, while Vicki drove alone separately. We talked about how she was feeling a form of grief for Tommy and expressing that grief through anger due to the frustration of not being able to really help Tommy get well. She was taking it out on Robyn because somehow she felt that Robyn was "holding her back," even though she was not. Mud was a person of action who wanted to "fix" things for the people she loved, but she couldn't "fix" Tommy. Everything about Tommy's health was out of her control (and ours), except our ability to pray for him.

We talked about doing all we could to give Tommy's condition to God, which would be a struggle for her (as it was for all of the rest of us). When she experienced anger, she needed to realize that it was a natural expression of grief and a symptom of needing to give Tommy's health back into God's hands.

Finally, I strongly defended Robyn. It was not Robyn's nature to ask for help, so Mud should not have that expectation of her. Rather, we needed to thank the good Lord that Robyn loved Tommy so much and was such a wonderful wife and caregiver to him. Hers was a role nobody else could fill. I told Mud that some spouses would leave home rather than face what Robyn had faced to stay with Tommy.

These were all strong words, delivered as lovingly as was possible by me, but still delivered directly. At the end, Mud agreed and said she had never looked at this anger as being a symptom of her grief.

Somehow I think this conversation really helped Mud, but I take no credit. I'm typically not so patient or thoughtful. I knew that God had answered my prayer, because Mud's tone changed radically over the next week or two. She was healing within herself, helped by God's hand.

A NEW DAY

Tommy didn't come home until January 18. It had been a rough few weeks, but he was in good spirits when he called that afternoon while waiting to be discharged.

"Today is the beginning of a new day," he said.

He also told me he had agreed to speak April 9 to a

breakfast sponsored by Workmatters, a faith-at-work ministry founded by our friend David Roth. Tommy was obviously optimistic and looking forward to better times.

About a week later, he brought up the speaking engagement again and said David had suggested he talk about relationships and servanthood.

"If you think I am any good at relationships, or if you have any ideas about what I should say," he said, "let's pray about it and talk about it."

My Journal, January 25, 2010

Most of Arkansas received a few inches of snow and ice, keeping some of us out of the office (or school) for a day or two. I thought about Tommy, wondering if he and Robyn were struggling with the thought that almost a year ago this kind of weather led to Tommy's tragic fall. I called Tommy to check on him. He quickly diffused my concern.

"It is a lovely day," he said. "This is the best snow we've had in years. I am sitting here by our fireplace, watching the snow fall in the backyard. I couldn't imagine a better situation."

Reflections: Seven Years Later

By Tommy Van Zandt

My immune system was not strong at all when I first returned to Fayetteville, and I pushed myself too far, too hard. Not a good combination.

I'd get in a routine of getting dressed, coming to the office, staying for three or four hours, going home, and having a routine there. And I'd be into the routine for a month or two, and then I'd get pneumonia or have to have surgery. It wasn't until my third year that my immune system was strong enough that I was able to stay out of the hospital for several months at a time.

That first year, I battled pneumonia for weeks at a time. And I had a pressure wound on my bottom because I pushed it too far. I'd go through weeks of lying only on one side and not being able to get in the wheelchair while trying to let it heal. It wouldn't heal, so eventually they did a surgical procedure. That required me to be in the hospital for around a month, only being able to see people from a bed and being on one side and getting turned every couple of hours. It was very frustrating, so that was definitely a down time.

It was really hard during those times when I couldn't work. I wanted to contribute financially —to provide for my family. That was part of it. But there was more to it than that.

I had helped build a company and the people in it. I'm very passionate about the company and the people. It gives me strength to be around them. And they were so incredibly patient and helpful. They wanted to help me get back in the office.

When you are passionate about something, whatever it is, you're going to push yourself to fill that need and fill that gap. I definitely wanted to be relevant. I didn't want to be a sick person or a crippled person; I wanted to be relevant in whatever way I could possibly do it. I wanted to be relevant as a spouse. As a father. As a friend. As a coworker.

By Robyn Van Zandt

I was so excited for Tommy to be back in Fayetteville, so excited for him to be home. He was so happy to be home, but it was crazy for months. There were times when he almost died. I found myself protecting Mark and Vicki and his mom a lot, just like I know there were times when they were protecting me and Tommy. We all had our own stuff to deal with, and we tried to protect other people, because you can only handle so much.

There was one pivotal moment in particular around the time they took out his gall bladder. Tommy looked at me, and he just said, "I am so sorry." You know how you, a husband and wife, can look at each other and understand things that are unsaid? Well, I could read beyond what he was saying.

That was the first time I ever thought he was to the point of thinking he didn't know if he was going to make it through this. Every other time, it was, "Bring it on. I'm doing it. I'm doing it." So that was really very, very hard.

Chapter 13

Tommy's New Life

"Neither this man nor his parents sinned," said Jesus, "but this
happened so that the works of God might be displayed in him."
JOHN 9:3 (NIV)

As you might expect, Tommy felt a great deal of pressure to work as much as possible. It's not easy for someone who's always worked hard and taken care of his family to suddenly feel dependent on the financial help of others. And while we admired and appreciated that quality in Tommy, we also knew that more work wasn't always in his best interest.

This was one of the topics Pat Carrigan and I discussed after Pat spent a weekend with the Van Zandts. And our discussion led to a series of e-mails with Tommy about priorities.

I made it clear we needed his help at Sage. But, I said, "You will have to make choices, and your health is the more pressing issue by a long shot." I pointed out our collective need to trust God, especially for the financial solutions. And I said getting and staying healthy was foundational to everything else he wanted to do, including working more and spending more time sharing his story.

Pat, who was copied on the e-mail, responded in support of what I had said.

"I hope you won't mind me weighing in on Mark's message," Pat wrote. "But heck, what are friends for, if not to stick their nose in your business?"

He reiterated many of the same points I had made and ended by saying Tommy could tell him to mind his own business. "But I may not listen!" he said. "Just love you guys too much." It was a totally heartfelt note.

ROAD TRIPS

Ross received a Dean's Scholarship to Texas Christian University that would pay part of his tuition. He also completed all of his financial aid applications, so he expected some additional help once those were processed.

I called to congratulate him, and we recalled our conversation back in September at Arsaga's coffee shop in Fayetteville. He had done exactly what I had advised, and he had done it on his own. He probably would have taken the same course of action whether or not we had ever had the conversation, but perhaps our talk had sharpened his resolve or added some sense of urgency. I told him we were proud of him.

John Mark, meanwhile, was preparing to marry Melissa Nutt in New Orleans on February 6. Tommy has been close to both John Mark and Marshall since they were babies, but it was not possible for Tommy to go to New Orleans. So Robyn planned to take the family to Fort Worth to TCU that weekend to give them something to look forward to in lieu of making the wedding.

It was a much shorter drive, but it still sounded

impractical to me. I said nothing in hopes that somehow she could pull it off. As it turned out, Tommy developed another red place on his skin on his rear end, so Robyn and the boys went to TCU without him.

Tommy never expressed that he felt sorry for himself that he could not go on either trip. Rather, in response to my request for help on my toast at the rehearsal dinner, he had his caregiver send me the following e-mail:

From: Tommy Van Zandt
Sent: Friday, February 05, 2010 1:24 PM
To: Mark Saviers
Subject: JM's toast
These are some words and terms that describe John Mark to me, starting as a baby to today:
Slobber, Drool, Toughness, Persistence, Grit, Good spirit, Leader, Melissa, Drool.
May God bless you both and your marriage. Wish we were there.
Love, Robyn and Tommy
Mark, this is pretty goofy. You can pick any of it that makes sense.

The wedding was fabulous in every way.

As we drove home exhausted on Sunday, February 7, I watched as the clock showed noon, and I thought about the fact that exactly one year ago at that moment Tommy had fallen off that ladder. I glanced several times into the back seat at Mud, who stared out the window in silence. None of us spoke a word about that awful anniversary, although I'm sure all of us thought about it.

Later, I learned that Ross had been one of two high school students who spoke that day at his church's "Youth

Sunday." It made me tear up to read the notes from his powerful speech, especially the end where he spoke about the Spring Break mission trip he took to Mexico just after Tommy was moved to Denver for rehab.

Youth Sunday, February 7, 2010, Ross Van Zandt (edited)

The past year has been the best and worst roller-coaster ride of my life. Exactly one year ago today, my dad fell off a ladder while attempting to cut broken limbs from a tree after the ice storm.

Panic ensued, but only for a moment. Then, as if the world were put on pause, everything stopped and I could feel the warmth of God around me. A picture of this plaque that my mom put in my room with Jeremiah 29:11 popped into my head: "For I know the plans I have for you, declares the LORD, plans to prosper you and not to harm you, plans to give you hope and a future." At that moment, heavenly calmness took over my body and I knew that no matter the physical damage, the Lord was not in it to harm our family.

Further reassurance came to me when the paramedics were wheeling my father away on the gurney and my dad, through all the pain, said to my little brother, Jack, "Jack, remember I can still beat you up!" To me he said, "Ross, get me some more of those technologies!" What that means, I have no clue, but his humor and huge smile assured me that everything was going to be alright.

We began to pray, this church began to pray, and the community began to pray. A month seemed like a year, as my dad slowly recovered and prepared for rehab while in the ICU at Washington Regional Hospital.

For now, he was a quadriplegic, but it took me a while to accept that. All I could think about was that past summer when my dad and I went to Jackson Hole, Wyoming, for a father-son retreat. And the image that seemed to never leave my head was of my almost-fifty-year-old dad climbing the mountain with me, with ease. All the other dads looked like they were going to call it quits and jump off the side of the mountain. To be honest, I was jealous of my dad's physical strength. How is it right for a lanky guy like me to have a buff, strong dad? The concept of him not being able to walk again was unbearable.

The year before (the accident), I went on the mission trip to Mexico and had the time of my life. Central Methodist sends two groups of high school students every Spring Break to a small town called Vicente Guerrero in the Baja of California. One group builds a house for a deserving family while the other helps out at an orphanage. God had it in His plan for me to attend the orphanage, even though I really wanted to go to the house build.

That first year, I was still a little immature and really focused on having the most fun I possibly could. Though I did have a blast, there was meaning to the trip when I discovered the need and poverty in the surrounding area. It was evident when we visited a migrant worker camp and fed the kids peanut butter and milk, because survival was the only thing that kept them going.

Yet those vehement desires fled at the hand of Christ. I helped a little girl come to Christ one night, and you could see the worries flee from her as she was certain that this worldly hell was not eternal; she would live eternally in Christ.

The second year, as thoughts of my dad's recovery filled my head, God prepared me in advance for the orphanage visit. He kept telling me to focus on the handicapped children. Sure enough, as soon as we arrived in Mexico last Spring Break, I immediately noticed how many handicapped children there really were. The year before, I had not even recognized that there were that many handicapped children.

How could the happiest people at the orphanage be the most physically and mentally disabled? God answered this question after a visit to one of the migrant worker camps.

God kept reassuring me and telling me to focus on the children. After doing a vacation Bible school type of lesson for the children at one of the camps, we fed the kids their peanut butter and filled their jars with milk. An older woman at the end of the line told the leader who came with us from the orphanage something. I could barely make out a few of the Spanish words. "Car ... hurt ... sick ... boy" is what I translated. I knew I must go and see the boy who was hurt, so I asked the leader if I could go with her to find the boy.

We were losing hope as we drove from shack to shack without any signs of the boy. God kept tugging at my heart to persevere and to find the boy, so I kept urging the leader to keep looking. We finally found the boy, mangled in his bed. It turns out that he was run over by a car, and his family couldn't afford to send him to the hospital in Ensenada along with his brother who was also run over. Yet, the mangled boy was at peace and was happy for his brother who was receiving treatment.

A Bible lay open next to his pillow as his mother wept at his bedside. We prayed for the boy and God gave me enough Spanish to tell him to not be afraid, for he was a strong son of God. He was at peace. His physical state was poor, yet his soul was rich with the Spirit and he was happy. He was probably going to die, yet he had the strength to know that he was in God's hands.

As I recollected the three disabled children that I met during my Spring Break experience at the orphanage while planning to speak in front of the Friday chapel service, I thought about my dad. Because God kept telling my heart to focus on the disabled children, I was able to learn that true happiness and the ability to minister to others is not hindered by physical or mental disabilities.

In fact, I learned it was the children who overcame the adversity in their lives who were strong, mature, wise, and filled with the Spirit. This taught me that maybe I should not be worried about my dad walking again. I should instead focus my energy on noticing the positives coming from the situation.

As soon as I was comforted by God's plan for my dad, I immediately saw the good stemming from our family's situation. My dad returned from Denver in September after seven months away, a new man. Though he was and still is unable to walk, he was the happiest I had ever seen him. He was thankful for the small things, and still is.

I now enjoy spending every moment of free time I have with him. We go for drives or listen to music or just talk. We have a stronger and closer relationship than we have ever had. He still cracks corny jokes and attempts to embarrass me in front of my friends, but true embarrassment is no longer possible because he is honestly the coolest person I know. I envy his patience and the happiness that radiates from his body, full of life, even though it still cannot physically move.

I encourage each and every one of you to listen to God's plan for you, to not be afraid of it, and to find true happiness in Christ our Lord. I know we all have our personal struggles and roadblocks, especially in these uncertain economic times, but we cannot focus on what we don't have. And to all the kids in the audience, don't wait for an accident or college to notice how cool your parents are, like I did. They really are awesome!

My Journal, February 13, 2010

Tommy and Robyn called to apologize for forgetting my birthday, which was four days ago. We laughed when Tommy blamed it on Robyn. I reminded him that this had happened most every year for the last forty-plus years, so it was hard to believe his old excuse of "your present is in the mail" was Robyn's fault.

Tommy's voice was clear and strong. He and Robyn sounded upbeat, even more than usual. I told Vicki that he seemed better than he had in a year. It made us feel wonderful that they were doing so well.

My Journal, February 18, 2010

When I started writing in this journal just over a year ago, I told someone I felt a little like Forrest Gump running from coast to coast. Like Forrest, I started because I felt a need to do it. Now, after a year, I feel tired and want to stop.

One reason I felt compelled to record these events was because I was sure God would help us in many ways, and I felt it was important to capture these interventions. Indeed, He has helped us! The miracles we have witnessed are numerous.

Looking back we have seen strength in many people, especially Robyn and Tommy, that is beyond "normal" and can only come from God. Many times we have felt inexplicable peace, even in very difficult circumstances.

We have seen many specific prayers answered. The Lord has brought us selfless, committed caregivers, both in the hospital and at home. When faced with dire financial needs, God has delivered unexpected help through friends and total strangers alike. Hundreds of people have contributed financially to the Van Zandt Family Trust or to making multiple Tommy's Nite Out events happen in both Dallas and Fayetteville. I will never forget the day Kim Butler from Dallas called us seemingly out of the blue more than six years after the first Tommy's Nite Out in Dallas and offered to put together another one there. It was held within a month or two of the date the family trust would have totally run out of money.

We have seen specific medical conditions healed, like skin problems or lung infections. We have seen friends or neighbors have a significant spiritual experience, inspired by reading the blog or through some other part of our story.

Another set of blessings has come from all of the new relationships, or rekindling of old relationships, that have come out of the last year. Vicki and I had heard for years about several close friends of Tommy and Robyn's in Dallas or Fayetteville. Now they are our friends too.

Old friends too numerous to name have risen up to help in their own unique way. We feel a bond to each of them now that supersedes the one we have always had.

Our family is even closer and stronger than we have ever been. Vicki and I know Ross and Jack much more deeply. Mud and I can talk about most anything now because we have needed to share our emotions or concerns almost daily for the past year. She is an amazing woman. Marshall, Beth, John Mark, and Melissa have thoughtfully helped weekly with Ross, Jack, and Mud.

When I reflect on all of these blessings of answered prayers, I am a bit overwhelmed with gratitude. The answers to prayer are all through this story and are easy to see. In fact, only one of my prayers remains unanswered as of this date. Almost daily I continue to ask the Lord to "turn on the switch" in Tommy's spine so that some relief from the paralysis will occur for him.

It is impossible not to mention this prayer, because so many have prayed for it for this whole year. Have we been praying for the wrong thing? How do we interpret the strange forecasts of healing by those spiritual women many months ago?

I do not know the answers to these questions. Maybe God's will is for His power to be made perfect in weakness (2 Corinthians 12:9). But I do know that some people will only use the measure of physical healing of the paralysis as a yardstick to determine if prayers really work. Many will shake their heads and walk away, thinking "poor Tommy." This is a mistake.

We know that God has orchestrated many, many miracles, because we have seen the answers to dozens of difficult prayer requests by thousands of people over this past year. Maybe the biggest is the peace and love that emanate from both Tommy and Robyn.

This story is not over. God is still working in us, and through us, every day. I look forward with great anticipation to see what God has in mind for Tommy, Robyn, Ross, Jack, and all of the rest of us. Whatever it is, we are at peace and we will accept His will. Thanks be to God and to Jesus Christ our Lord.

REFLECTIONS: EIGHT YEARS LATER

A Q&A with Tommy and Robyn Van Zandt

Question: Tommy, you mentioned in an earlier reflection that you never felt like giving up. Robyn, how about you? Did you have moments when you wanted to give up?

Robyn: I am often very disappointed that Tommy and I are not able to have the life that we were hoping to have once the children were out on their own. Many times I am frustrated that Tommy's dependence is like having a small child again. Selfishly I want my time to be my time and not have to be responsible for the welfare of another person. However, I don't know what giving up would look like. How do you give up on thirty years with someone who means so much to you? How could I do that to Tommy? How could I do that to my children? How could I do that to me?

Question: Why were you able to have such hope?

Robyn: Several reasons. I made a vow to God, Tommy, and myself when I married Tommy. Also, when we had children, it was no longer just about the two of us.

I am extremely thankful Tommy is the kind of person who does not fall into self-pity, dragging everyone down into despair with him. Neither is he an angry, self-indulgent person. He is actually the opposite. He is still funny, kind, smart, and wants to help and lift others up. I know that if he could he would do anything for me, so he is an example to me of the meaning of sacrifice. Sometimes I am aware that I am making a sacrifice; however, most of the time it does not feel like sacrifice—I get to spend time with him.

Question: What advice would you give someone going through a tragedy?

Tommy: I have said many times that without my faith I would have never made it. I would talk to this person about their faith, if any. If they are a believer in Jesus, I would pursue that deeper with them. If not, I would advise them to seek spiritual guidance from someone like close family, friends, or clergy. Tragedy is not a journey you can take alone. Realize the horrible situation you may be in at the moment, but appropriately seek a way forward.

Robyn: As simple as this sounds, you have to take it one day at a time. Some days it is one moment at a time. It is crushing, overwhelming, emotionally exhausting, frustrating, scary, and confusing. Allow others to minister to you, but also be OK with having your boundaries. Sometimes very loving, well-meaning people have no idea how tired and overwhelmed you are and how you cannot be available to answer questions. It is not aloofness. It is protection as you sort out what is going on. CaringBridge.org is a wonderful way to update those who care about what is happening to you or your family, and having a very close friend or family member updating others is most helpful.

Question: In what ways is life better for you now?

Tommy: My life is much better with regard to my stronger relationship with Jesus. I am much more aware of those around me and want to understand what is going on in their lives. I was always a people person, but I was too ADD and "too busy" to say hello to people at the mall, in a grocery store, etc. I now choose to project a smile and sense of joy as often as possible. Unfortunately, Robyn and some of my closest caregivers see a more impatient side. I truly regret these instances, because they are the most important people in my life.

Robyn: I don't know if I would consider life better than before, but it has more meaning and I have more perspective. When you are faced with losing someone over and over, as I was for the first two years after Tommy's accident, you realize just how much that person really means to you. The fact that Tommy's voice is the same and his personality and spirit are intact is the most important thing.

Our marriage has not been perfect; in fact, we have been challenged in many different ways. But our history is extremely important. No one knows my family as much as he does, no one has experienced me at my best and at my worst like Tommy has, and he still loves me more than himself. We have experienced the good and the challenges that life has to offer.

We also have had the privilege of seeing people

at their best. Tommy's family dropping everything to help us through this sudden tragedy, willing to change their life to take care of our boys. We continue to be amazed at our friends and even people we do not know who want to help us financially so we can take care of Tommy's needs at home.

Tommy's accident put into focus how much more meaningful relationships are over anything else. Knowing that life can change in an instant magnifies how precious life is, the importance of forgiveness, that the present is all that really matters, and that people are so much more valuable than things.

Question: What's your ministry now and how is it growing?

Tommy: I've had many opportunities over the years to meet with people previously unknown to me about their life struggles and discuss with them where they are in their faith journey. This wheelchair and my story attracts people to me. I think God brings people to me who have a need I can possibly help with.

I think that is my ministry with a particular focus on individuals and smaller groups. I like to see people eye to eye and really try to feel what is going on within their hearts and minds. That is difficult to do with larger groups. I don't mind large groups periodically, but it is not my comfort zone. I think God has blessed me with the ability to listen more intently now than ever before, so I truly think I can make a difference in some people's lives.

I now understand why God has put us on this earth—to "love your God with all your heart, mind and soul. Love your neighbors as yourself." Everyone we come in contact with on a daily basis is our "neighbor." Hopefully, I can spread that in my own way.

Robyn: I started a Life Coaching business because I have always been fascinated with personal growth. I came to the conclusion that my training in counseling and coaching, as well as my life experiences, are valuable in helping others who may feel confused, emotionally paralyzed, or fearful to move forward or make a change. I am very interested in how people perceive their personal history, their present circumstances, and how it is possible to change limiting perspectives to give a person hope and meaning moving forward.

We are still working through how to reach out to other people who want to hear our message of transcending paralysis, whether it is physical, emotional, or spiritual. If people are interested in connecting with us about speaking about our experiences, we are open to that option.

Question: What else would you like to share?

Robyn: We are all loved, and life still has plenty to offer that is good. So spending too much time on the "what ifs" just steals the joy of the present. We are definitely planted in reality and have our sad, frustrating moments, but all in all, we are acutely aware of our blessings.

I know I am a different person as a result of all that has happened over the last thirty years of my life of being with Tommy. He was a gift then and is a gift now. He may look and act differently, but he is enough. I am enough and you are enough. Revel in that. Be profoundly grateful for what you do have and believe that whatever comes into your life, you are not alone. There is hope, and your life matters.

Tommy: By God's grace, I am still here. And by His grace, we are all here for a reason. Every day is a blessing. Use it wisely. You never know when your life may get "flipped"!

November 2017

While turning my old journal notes into this book several years after the actual events, I am overwhelmed with thankfulness. In the first year after Tommy's accident, none of our family could imagine that our lives could return to this state of normalcy. Granted, we have a "new normal," but a life full of blessings nonetheless.

During those darkest hours, we all had our fears. Many of my fears from that time are reflected in this book. After reading a draft of this manuscript, Ross pointed out that he had imagined scenarios where he would need to live at home as a caregiver instead of going to college. Today, Ross is an honor's graduate from TCU, enjoying his dream job at an advertising firm in Dallas.

Jack is also doing well today, working and enjoying his life in Fayetteville. He and Ross are still very close. Jack has said that every time he feels like life is a struggle, he thinks of his dad and is inspired to press forward.

Robyn has launched a new career as a life coach, which draws not only on her educational background, but also on her life experiences. Her goal is to "give back" to others who are going through times of transition. She takes care of Tommy every day.

Tommy lives at home with Robyn, where he always wanted to be, in Fayetteville, Arkansas. He still works at Sage Partners, our commercial real estate firm. It takes about four hours each morning to feed, shower, medically prepare, and dress him to get him ready for work—and almost that much time to get him ready for bed at night. But almost every afternoon, when health permits, he is at the office contributing to the company and the community.

He and Robyn inspire hundreds of people, including me. Tommy regularly speaks to groups in the community who call on him. You can learn more about Tommy today at www.flippedstory.com.

Tommy could not live at home, and perhaps would not be alive today, without the generosity of friends. The $20,000 to $22,000 per month in excess of their income for twenty-four-hour in-home care and other expenses needed to sustain him is raised at fundraisers every year or two, still labeled Tommy's Nite Out. The proceeds of this book will be contributed to the Van Zandt Family Trust.

We will continue to question our health-care system for people like Tommy. Why does our health-care system encourage quadriplegics to live in a nursing home, rather than at home, in order to obtain financial help? It is clear that most, including Tommy, can live much more productive lives at home. When compared to living in a nursing home, it seems that living at home is much more cost-effective.

And we continue to have hope. While Tommy is generally healthier, he has had no recovery in his mobility. I personally believe that perhaps the visions some had for recovery from his paralysis are beautiful pictures of Tommy in eternity. I look forward to the day the two of us can jump up together and do a chest bump in heaven.

When I asked Tommy, more than seven years after the accident, how he felt about the early visions of recovery from paralysis, his answer was immediate: "We took those very seriously. I count them as huge blessings. At the time, I was in a fight to get something back, and I was in a fight for my life. I wouldn't be alive today without all of the prayers and positive thoughts about being healed. I can't believe all of the time people took to pray for me and be with me."

David Twiford, the brother of our friend Rainer Twiford, wrote this to me after reading a draft of this book: "Jesus looks at us and sees our soul, not our physical appearance. He sees Tommy as a completed soul who happens to have a body. He doesn't need to heal Tommy's physical infirmities to prove anything, because He has looked into Tommy's heart and soul. While He cares about our infirmities, He is assured that Tommy already knows Him, His power, and His love and needs no further proof."

I love David's insights here, because he takes an eternal view of the way Jesus sees Tommy. When I think deeply about it, I know it's also the way Jesus sees each of us. This perspective helps me try to change the way I view other people—flipping my natural focus on their outward appearance and, instead, focusing on each person's heart and soul. I often fail, but Jesus is helping daily to transform me.

This has allowed us to thank God for the many blessings He has bestowed upon us. Some are reflected in this book, and many others are not. Words can't reflect our gratitude for the people and support and strength that God has brought to us. And He continues to bring those blessings to us daily. As Ross so aptly stated in a recent note to me, "Life is good, and God is good."

Acknowledgments

This recollection of events in this book would not have been possible without the diligent work of my assistant and friend, Cindy Green. Cindy not only typed or corrected the original journal (and many revisions), she also helped accumulate the many reference materials. In addition, she has logged every donation to the Van Zandt Family Trust and generated thank-you notes to each one. All of this work was done on top of a full-time list of duties required in her daily job in our commercial real estate business. We appreciate you so much, Cindy. Thank you from all of us.

For several years after these events were recorded, I wavered many times about whether it should actually be turned into a book. The nagging question in my mind was "Who would want to read it?" One of my very dear friends and business partners, Marc Myers, convinced me this story was indeed compelling and that I should publish it. In fact, he ordered the first ten copies in advance. Marc, thanks for the encouragement.

Turning my journal notes into a comprehensible book was a daunting task. We prayed for help, and it came in the form of Stephen Caldwell. Stephen calls himself a ghostwriter, but his talents were critical. He has become a friend in the process. He reduced the normal fee to do this work because, as a dedicated follower of Jesus, he wanted to help tell this story.

When the manuscript was further along in editing, my next doubt was "Is this good enough?" Two people in particular coached me along and encouraged me—Steve Graves and Elise Mitchell. Both are very accomplished business leaders and authors. After answering tons of my questions, both concluded with a table-pounding challenge: Finish the book!

Ashley and Kurt Knickrehm regularly expressed interest in the creation of this book, so I shared an early draft with them. They took the time to list their comments and posed a lot of questions—especially related to what Robyn and Tommy were thinking and feeling during the events reflected in my journal. This led to significant expansion of the "Reflections" at the end of each chapter. Thank you, Ashley and Kurt. Now we are all blessed by what Robyn and Tommy have shared.

Finally, we want to thank all the family members and friends who have supported us through this journey. There are too many to list by name. Some are mentioned in the book, and many others aren't. But your letters, e-mails, texts, and gracious displays of love helped shape our family's story and this book. We literally couldn't have written it without you.

Mark Saviers
on behalf of
Tommy and Robyn Van Zandt

If you would like to learn more about the Van Zandt family, donate to the Van Zandt Family Trust, or if your own life has been "flipped" and you are seeking resources, please visit flippedstory.com.

P.46 Mapping the Finances
7, 8 (48-VIII - P56)
P 63